Real Matter

For Ed,

a greeting from across
the continent,

a thank you for (nearly)
four decades of friendship,

David

april 6, 1997

DAVID ROBERTSON

Real Matter

The University of Utah Press   Salt Lake City

MAPS BY JACOB P. MANN

The 1954, 1955, and 1956 journals of Gary Snyder and material from interviews with Gary Snyder are quoted with permission of Gary Snyder.

Material from the interview with Philip Whalen is quoted with permission of Philip Whalen.

"On Climbing the Sierra Matterhorn Again After Thirty-one Years" by Gary Snyder is reproduced by permission of the author. "The Circumambulation of Mt. Tamalpais," by Gary Snyder, is reproduced with permission of Gary Snyder and Counterpoint Press.

"Opening the Mountain, Tamalpais: 22:X:65," by Philip Whalen is reproduced with permission of Philip Whalen.

Different versions of chapter 1 appeared in *West of Eden: A History of the Art and Literature of Yosemite,* © 1984 by the Yosemite Association and Wilderness Press, and *Yosemite As We Saw It: A Centennial Collection of Early Writings and Art,* © 1990 by the Yosemite Association.

A different version of chapter 2 appeared in *Yosemite* 54:4 (1988), © by Yosemite Association.

A different version of chapter 2 appeared in the fourth issue of *Wild Duck Review* (1995), © by *Wild Duck Review.*

Chapter 3 appeared in *San Jose Studies* 21:1–3 (1995), © 1995 by San Jose State University. The chapter "Side Trip" appeared in *Terra Nova* 1:2 (1996), © 1996 by MIT Press.

Chapter 4 appeared in *Western American Literature* 27:3 (1992), © 1992 by Utah State University.

Chapter 5 appeared in *Western American Literature* 30:1 (1995), © 1995 by Utah State University.

Library of Congress Cataloging-in-Publication Data
Robertson, David, 1937–
    Real matter / David Robertson
        p.   cm.
    Includes bibliographical references (p.   ).
    ISBN 0-87480-533-3 (cloth : alk. paper). — ISBN 0-87480-534-1 (paper : alk. paper)
    1. West (U.S.)—Description and travel. 2. California—Description and travel.
3. Robertson, David, 1937–   —Journeys—West (U.S.) 4. Robertson, David, 1937–
—Journeys—California. 5. Hiking—California. 6. Automobile travel—West (U.S.)
7. Travelers' writings, American—West (U.S.)—History and criticism. 8. Travelers'
writings, American—California—History and criticism.   I. Title.
F595.3.R634   1997
917.804—dc21   95-50029
                                                                                CIP

"The closer you get to real matter,

rock air fire wood, boy, the more

spiritual the world is."

Japhy Ryder in

JACK KEROUAC, *Dharma Bums*

Contents

Preface ix

Acknowledgments xi

1 · A SECRET AT THE
HEART OF THE UNIVERSE

Location of the Secret 2

Content of the Secret 8

Wild Heart 17

2 · VALUE IN MOUNTAINS

Tracking Clarence King
  through Space and Time 26

You Can't Fall Off Mountains 35

Tracking Moses on His Way
  to Sinai 42

Photographic Reclimb 46

3 · LOST BORDERS

The Mesa Trail 54

Saturated with the Elements 59

The Language of the Hills 62

Mrs. Walker 65

The Soundness of Nature 68

SIDE TRIP: THE LONELIEST
ROAD IN AMERICA

The Road 78

Fences 81

The Terrain 83

Nowhere 85

Home Farm 87

Mt. Moriah 90

4 · THE CLOSER YOU
GET TO REAL MATTER

Real Matter 100

The Practice 101

The Hike 104

Dharma Bum 107

Beat Christian 111

Hershey Bars 113

5 · COMING ROUND
THE MOUNTAIN

Before 122

Stages 1–10 123

After 138

6 · REAL MATTER, REAL SELF

Real Self 148

Unreal Self 149

With Moses on Mt. Sinai 150

Heroes on Vision Quests 152

Honeymoon in the Sinai Desert 154

Appendixes 161

Literature Cited 171

Index 175

The closer we came to the town of Independence in California's Owens Valley, the more I realized I did not know how to write about Mary Austin. Austin lived in Independence and other towns in Owens Valley for a few years around the turn of the century and wrote two books about the valley that I liked very much, *Land of Little Rain* and *Lost Borders.* She had to go in my book. The question was, how to do it.

The book was about writers who go on trails and come back to write about their experiences. I knew then most of the writers I wanted to include. Fitz Hugh Ludlow in Yosemite in 1863, Clarence King range hopping from the Great Western Divide to the crest of the Sierra Nevada in 1864, Gary Snyder and Jack Kerouac on Yosemite's Matterhorn Peak in 1955, the same two on Mt. Tamalpais in 1956, and the threesome of Gary Snyder, Allen Ginsberg, and Philip Whalen doing a circumambulation of Mt. Tamalpais in 1965. I would put all these latter-day hikers in historical perspective by going back to Moses and the Israelites trekking across the Sinai Desert.

I even knew that I wanted one chapter to be different from the rest. I would put it right in the middle of the book. In all the other chapters I would hike in some famous writer's footsteps, keep a journal, take photographs, and integrate my notes and my photographs with some literary history and literary criticism. In the middle chapter, however, I would go off on my own. Not only that, I would take a highway instead of a trail. And it would not be to the top of a mountain. It would be my favorite section of one of America's greatest roads, Highway 50 through the heart of Nevada. That would also mean that I would go out of state. All the other routes were in California. I wanted to do this chapter for contrast. I wanted to know what I would see when by myself on a way that did not go to a summit. What would happen when I went up and down between two arbitrary points, Nevada's borders with California and Utah?

But we were on Highway 395, not Highway 50, and the issue was Mary

Austin. Mark Hoyer was driving. He was writing a dissertation on Austin and the Paiute people of Owens Valley and wanted to do some on-site research. I remembered how helpful Mark had been when I could not get the chapter on the circumambulation of Mt. Tamalpais organized. "Make the chapter itself into a circumambulation," he suggested. Which I did. So, as we coasted the Sherwin Grade into the town of Bishop, where Austin also lived briefly, I admitted, "I can't figure out how to get Austin into my *Real Matter* book." Mark replied with a suggestion so simple that I knew immediately it was right, "Since your book is about trails, why don't you use the "Mesa Trail" chapter of *Land of Little Rain*?"

Acknowledgments

The first thank-yous go to Jeannette Robertson and Sean O'Grady, because they said I could make a book out of what I thought was only a handful of hikes. The next thank-you goes to Mark Hoyer, who rescued two of these chapters from considerable disorder. After that comes round upon round of people. In what is surely a futile effort not to leave out someone, I have picked out some categories. There are the people who accompanied me on hikes: Sean O'Grady again, Eric Paul Shaffer, Andrew Kirk, Chris Ransick, Mark Hoyer, Stephanie Sarver, Katrina Schimmoeller, Chris Sindt, Frederica Bowcutt, Melissa Nelson, Maryann Owens, D Jones, Harold Glasser, Mark Wheelis, Bruce Hammock, Vince Crockenberg, Paul Noel, Valerie Cohen, and Michael Cohen. Hal Faulkner gets thanked because he was on the Matterhorn hike and because he helped me see the way a camera does. Other photographers I am particularly indebted to are Ted Orland and Jerry Uelsmann. David Rothenberg gets thanked because he was on the Moriah hike and because he edited "Side Trip" for *Terra Nova*. Tom Lyon, editor of *Western American Literature,* I thank because he originally turned down chapter 5 and thereby eventually made it much better. In the category of editors also goes Casey Walker of *Wild Duck Review,* who helped me rearrange chapter 2. In the English department at the University of California at Davis are Joyce Wade, Peter Dale, Karl Zender, and Jack Hicks. In the Program in Comparative Literature is Scott McLean. At Yosemite are Dave Forgang, Norma Craig, Barbara Beroza, Steve Medley, Linda Eade, and Jim Snyder. In Independence is the staff of the Eastern California Museum. Then there are the people who granted me interviews: Val Taylor and John B. Free at Home Farm and Richard Moreno in Carson City. And the last are equal to the first: thank you to Gary Snyder and Philip Whalen for helping me see.

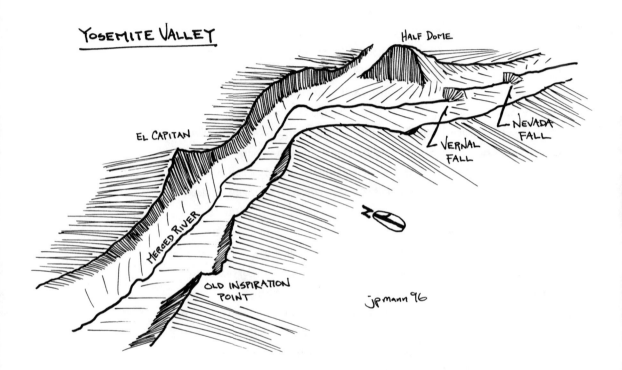

YOSEMITE VALLEY

HALF DOME

EL CAPITAN

VERNAL FALL

NEVADA FALL

MERCED RIVER

OLD INSPIRATION POINT

N

jpmann 96

CHAPTER ONE

A Secret at the Heart of the Universe

LOCATION OF THE SECRET

During the summer of 1863 the East Coast intellectual and writer Fitz Hugh Ludlow entered Yosemite Valley at the conclusion of a transcontinental journey with the painter Albert Bierstadt. Six years earlier Ludlow had gained notoriety with the publication of *The Hasheesh Eater,* a chronicle of his experiences as a drug addict, and by 1863 patrons of the arts had begun to note how grandly Bierstadt presented on canvas the monumental scenery of the American West. Their trip overland to California was designed to solidify their emerging reputations by giving Ludlow new material to write about and Bierstadt bold new vistas to paint. Ludlow sent accounts of their journey to the *Atlantic Monthly* and later gathered the published articles together in a book entitled *The Heart of the Continent.*

Like most visitors in the years immediately following the discovery of the valley by white Americans in 1851, the Ludlow-Bierstadt party followed an Indian trail that led from the town of Mariposa through the meadows at Wawona to a place high on the south rim now called Old Inspiration Point. From this platform, 3,000 feet above the western end of the valley, Ludlow thought that he had arrived in paradise shortly after its creation:

> Our dense leafy surrounding hid from us the fact of our approach to the Valley's tremendous battlement, till our trail turned at a sharp angle and we stood on "Inspiration Point." That name had appeared pedantic, but we found it only the spontaneous expression of our own feelings on the spot. We did not so much seem to be seeing from that crag of vision a new scene on the old familiar globe as a new heaven and new earth into which the creative spirit had just been breathed. (Ludlow 1864, 746)

After describing for his readers the great walls of granite enclosing this "Scripture of Nature" (746), he turned his attention to the valley floor. He noted that to the west it opened out into broad canyons that led to the vast field of light of the San Joaquin Valley. To the east, however, it "narrow[ed] to a little strait of green between the butments that uplift the giant domes" (748). The meadows below Inspiration Point gradually gave way to "a dense wood of cedars, oaks, and pines," and finally even these hardy specimens disappeared in an amphitheater of lifeless crag, where "not a living creature, either man or beast, br[oke] the visible silence" (748). Responding to the constriction and eventual enclosure of the valley, as well as to the harshness of the landscape he saw in the distance, Ludlow's thoughts became morbid. Yosemite at its eastern end seemed a closet where a guilt-ridden Nature had retreated to brood on the consequences of its cataclysmic acts. He and his companions were intruders who might unintentionally be punished for their audacity:

> We were breaking into the sacred closet of Nature's self-examination.
> What if, on considering herself, she should of a sudden, and us-ward
> unawares, determine to begin the throes of a new cycle,—spout up
> remorseful lavas from her long-hardened conscience, and hurl us all
> skyward in a hot concrete with her unbosomed sins? (748)

Later in their Yosemite sojourn Ludlow and fellow trespassers dared to open the door of the inner sanctum at the valley's eastern end. They left their camp in the broad meadow below Yosemite Falls to explore the upper reaches of the main fork of the Merced River. Horses carried them the first three miles; after that they had to proceed on foot. The going was difficult. In some places they were "compelled to squeeze sideways through a narrow crevice in the rocks"; in others they "became quadrupedal, scrambling up acclivities with which the bald main precipice had made but slight compromise" (752). But they persevered, making their way through the narrows below Vernal Fall, then to the top of the fall by means of ladders placed there a few years earlier, and finally to the bottom of Nevada Fall. There they faced a seemingly insurmountable wall. Nature would permit no further intrusion:

A Secret
at the Heart
of the Universe

> At the base of Yo-wi-ye [Nevada Fall] we seem standing in a *cul-de-sac* of Nature's grandest labyrinth. Look where we will, impregnable battlements hem us in. (753)

If only they could get out of the closeted canyon to the heights above, rather astounding revelations awaited them:

> Eight hundred feet above us, could we climb there, we should find the silent causes of power. There lie the broad, still pools that hold the reserved affluence of the snow-peaks; thence might we see, glittering like diamond lances in the sun, the eternal snow-peaks themselves. . . . Even from Inspiration Point, where our trail first struck the battlement, we could see far beyond the Valley to . . . the everlasting snow-forehead of Castle Rock [identity unclear], his crown's serrated edge cutting the sky at the topmost height of the Sierra. We had spoken of reaching him,—of holding converse with the King of all the Giants. (753–754)

Such a conversation was not to be. In his disappointment, Ludlow came to a weary conclusion:

> This whole weary way have we toiled since then,—and we know better now. Have we endured all these pains only to learn still deeper Life's saddest lesson,—"Climb forever, and there is still an Inaccessible"? (754)

The symphonic poem of Ludlow's experience in Yosemite consisted of two movements. The theme of the first movement went down and in. The metaphor of closet was the leitmotif. From Inspiration Point the walls of the valley seemed to close upon an unseen point, a place where Nature sequestered itself to ponder the dark secrets of its creation. The walls themselves were defenses it erected against human discovery of those secrets. The second movement went in the opposite direction, up and out. Even from Inspiration Point Ludlow could see that the valley of the Merced led not to constricted caverns dark within the earth, but to the open spaces and bright light of the high mountains. That is the destination he and his companions truly desired. There, if they could only reach it, they would find the "silent causes of power." Conversation with the "King" who abides there would surely disclose secrets worth knowing. But in actual experience they found the sublime inaccessible.

Ludlow's narrative is the most fully developed statement of a theme common to many other authors of the time. To Yosemite came travel writers and reporters from Britain (such as W. H. Russell) and from the east coast of the United States (such as Albert Richardson), tourists who later became famous (such as Ansel Adams), and tourists who never became famous (such as O. W. Lehmer, Emilie Sussman, William Baer, L. E. Danley, and one of my favorites, Cora Morse), whose writings are put away in library closets unless a researcher like myself retrieves them. That these people and many others like them, from such diverse educational and occupational backgrounds, continuously recapitulate Yosemite's "secret" theme testifies to its imaginative power.

The idea that Yosemite's mammoth rocks were Nature's fortress against unwonted inspection was particularly popular. Lehmer asserted that at the doorway to Yosemite "mighty sentinels guard the entrance" (n.d., n.p.). Chief among the sentinels, according to Sussman, was El Capitan, "a huge rock standing out far into the valley," which "seems to try to guard it from all trespassers" (1872, 4). Russell made the connection with keeping secrets explicit: "The peculiar and unique features of the valley seem to me to be the height and the boldness of the cliffs which spring out from the mountain-sides like sentinels to watch and ward over the secrets of the gorge" (1902, 29–30). If Yosemite visitors could only manage to slip past the guards into Nature's hideout, they would arrive in a very special place. Baer thought of this place as kin to Ludlow's closet. He felt that he and his companions, who arrived in Yosemite seven years before Ludlow in only the second season of tourist travel, "appeared like intruders into the realm of Nature's secret repose" (Baer 1856). Other writers used images reminiscent of the second movement of Ludlow's symphony. Richardson, when he arrived on Inspiration Point three years after Ludlow, thought that "Nature had lifted her curtain to reveal the vast and the infinite" (1867, 422). Lehmer directed his readers, if they would truly "appreciate the wonders of Yosemite," to go to the place Ludlow tried to reach, "the awesome heights where the majesty of the Infinite sits enthroned on rock and snow." But, in harmony with Ludlow's theme of disillusionment, he felt it necessary to warn his readers that, once there, they will find other mountains "drifting away," like Ludlow's Inaccessible, "into that hazy distance which wraps in impenetrable mystery the mountain solitudes of the world" (n.d., n.p.).

In perhaps the most interesting permutation of Ludlow's controlling metaphor of the Merced Canyon as an ever narrowing closet, a few writers thought of Yosemite not as a room within a house, but as a heart within a body. For Danley and many others, Yosemite was the heart of the Sierra Nevada. Arriving by train in El Portal in 1908, headed for "the snow-capped Sierras that rose abruptly before" him, he wondered if he could possibly "penetrate to their very heart in this comfortable manner" (Danley 1908, 18). Ansel Adams made the body bigger. He believed that Yosemite was at the heart of the entire earth: "The great rocks of Yosemite, expressing qualities of timeless, yet intimate grandeur, are the most compelling formation of their kind. We should not casually pass them by for they are the very heart of the earth speaking to us" (1949, foreword). Morse made the body within which Yosemite beats no smaller than the cosmos itself. "Ah Yosemite!" she declared in a statement that summarizes in a single phrase the complex of ideas Ludlow expressed more fully, "Thy heart holds the secret of the Universe" (1896, 7).

These authors believed that Yosemite is so situated, not just on but more importantly in the body of the earth, that it records the earth's natural waves of meaning. Visitors to the park can put their ears to its granite and hear the planet whisper its inmost thoughts. In addition, for some of them, like

Morse, Yosemite also has truly cosmic connections. There used to be a sign along the southside drive into the heart of Yosemite Valley. It advised motorists what frequency on their car radios would give them road and weather information. Morse might well have wanted it replaced by another sign, one that read: Adjust Your Heartset to Yosemite's Beat "until the thrill of the pulse of the universe is felt and appreciated" (25).

Almost all early visitors to Yosemite shared a belief in the religious significance of the natural landscape. They also agreed that the religious knowledge held by landscape is not obvious, nor is the spiritual power it contains immediately available. So they whispered the word "secret," again and again. While they were not equally optimistic about the ability of human beings to locate this secret, all tacitly assumed that access to remote place equals access to secret. Hence, the importance of exploration if the way is not known, and the importance of trails once the way is known. Trails make it easier to get there if the going is difficult, and they make it possible to follow others who have gone there before. No need for everyone to reinvent the way.

CONTENT OF THE SECRET

Nineteenth-century visitors such as Fitz Hugh Ludlow and Cora Morse believed that people might go to Yosemite to learn a very important secret, maybe even the secret of the universe itself. What a good idea, I thought. What, do you suppose, is the secret?

Perhaps some of these very travellers had found it. So I returned to the Yosemite library, where I had read their books in the first place, and delved deeper. I found nothing helpful. Ludlow himself had nothing more to say on the subject. Other writers did, but they were vague and illusive, sometimes doing nothing more than making a string of beads out of abstract nouns. Listening to the beat of the "heart of the earth," Ansel Adams heard no words more definite than "spirit and beauty" (foreword). So formidable was the task of stating the content of the secret that Richardson gave up, oppressed:

> Nature had lifted her curtain to reveal the vast and the infinite. It elicited no adjectives, no exclamations. With bewildering sense of divine power and human littleness, I could only gaze in silence, till the view strained my brain and pained my eyes, compelling me to turn away and rest from its oppressive magnitude. (1867, 422)

At this point it seemed best to leave the library and try to learn Yosemite's secrets by opening the closet door myself. Retracing Ludlow's very route seemed a good plan and would be easy to do. A modern highway would take me straight from the San Joaquin Valley right into the middle of Yosemite Valley in no more than two hours. Then, a veritable freeway of a trail would take me past the place where he felt walled in and give me ready access to Yosemite's high backcountry. Ludlow's contemporaries were not long content with being stymied by the sheer four-hundred-foot drop of Nevada Fall. Early on, trails that skirted this "cul-de-sac" were built to provide access to what he considered "Inaccessible." They were forerunners of the John Muir Trail, which was conceived on a 1914 outing of the Sierra

Club and built in the years immediately thereafter as a cooperative effort of the National Park Service, the Forest Service, and the state of California. It takes the hiker from Yosemite Valley into the Yosemite high country and then beyond to the Sierra Nevada's Pinnacle of Inaccessibility, Mt. Whitney.

So, in the spring of 1981 I loaded my hulk of a Travelall with supplies and drove south down Highway 99 from the Sacramento area. At Manteca I turned east out of the flatland of the San Joaquin Valley and rode State Highway 140 up and down the foothills of the Sierra Nevada like an old seesaw. An hour later I slowed down for the old mining town of Mariposa, where the sign reassured me that the route was "Open." After Midpines Summit, some seven miles down the road, Highway 140 took a long, winding dip to the Merced River and then followed it to El Portal. Here, back before an all-weather road from Mariposa was completed, was where passengers on the Yosemite Railroad exchanged "cars." It was the end of the rail and the beginning of the road. Promoters probably named it El Portal to echo El Capitan. Today, it is a bedroom community for government employees and a motel refuge for visitors who cannot find lodging in the valley. I drove through at 55 mph.

A real gateway was a few miles up the road, and it had double doors. First a stop at the official entrance station, where a uniformed ranger took a $3.00 initiation fee. A dark, natural tunnel of rock just beyond seemed to be a spiritual El Portal, a birth canal leading from everyday life to the magical geography of granite on the other side. The next ten miles were negotiable by car, mostly down a one-way road past turnouts where I stopped momentarily to view El Capitan and Yosemite Falls. Eventually I arrived at Curry Village, where I had to park the Travelall in an old apple orchard planted in the 1850s, whose fruit nowadays is eaten mostly by bears. A National Park Service shuttle bus took me through the forest to Happy Isles, where a sign told me to cross the bridge over the Merced River to the beginning of the John Muir Trail. The bridge seemed to separate mainland Yosemite from some other place, perhaps the place where the secret was kept. Ever since I had left the expansive San Joaquin Valley I had felt my way narrowing. Ludlow had noticed the same phenomenon. The walls kept pushing in closer, as if I were

A Secret
at the Heart
of the Universe

being funnelled across this bridge. I was being forced to slow down—from a car to a bus to a walk. I walked across the bridge.

June 10, 1981   Yosemite Lodge
Leave the domestic behind, the sign said, as I started up the John Muir Trail this morning:

> *No Pets Allowed on Trails*

This hike is hazardous:

> *Warning—Danger*
> *Ice and Rock*
> *Frequently Fall on Trail*
> *Hikers Assume*
> *Their Own Risk*

I looked around. The place seemed safe enough. Where was this dangerous desti-nation? A few more feet and my question was answered. A sign, this one quoting the trail's namesake, John Muir, let me know what my ultimate destination was:

> *As long as I live*
> *I'll hear waterfalls and birds and winds sing.*
> *I'll interpret the rocks,*
> *Learn the language of the flood, storm, and*
> *the avalanche.*
> *I'll acquaint myself with the glaciers and wild*
> *gardens,*
> *and get as near the heart of the world as I can.*

I felt good, especially when I read "heart of the world." It reminded me of what I had read by Danley, Adams, and Morse. I was right to leave the library. A sign nearby looked as if it were put there to gloss "the heart of the world" and provide the first unmistakable hint of the secret's content:

> *Each step along this trail*
> *is a step away from the road*
> *a step closer to wilderness.*

So that's where I was headed. *Apparently what was in danger was my civilized self.*

Now that I knew where I was going, the question was, How do I get there? More signs along the way made it clear that I had to do more than follow the crumbling asphalt trail that lay at my feet. They seemed to think I was pretty uptight. Sharpen those senses that urban living has dulled!

Fragrant laurel leaves.

Can you find them?

and

Listen

to water sounds

changing with each step.

Other signs addressed my ignorance. Understand, they preached, the deep structures of the Yosemite wilderness, how it came to be and how it changes. It's all one intelligible process. Science will be your instructor. Successive signs diagrammed and explained "Rounded Scenery," "Angular Scenery," "Master Joints," and "Crumbling Mountains."

I crossed a handsome wooden bridge over the Merced River below Vernal Fall. A whole battery of new signs hit me in the face:

Caution

Emergency Telephone

Stay on Trail

Stay Alive

More doom. It looked as if crossing the bridge had upped the ante. A few more steps and it was back to John Muir, the eponymous ancestor of all who press on past danger. A sign that turned out to be the next to last one quoted his most famous lines. I knew them by heart:

When we try to pick out anything by itself,

We find it hitched to everything else

in the universe.

Then the final sign. Deep in the live-oak shade, patches of sunlight allowed me to read the words. It addressed me directly:

You have taken the first step to wilderness.
The next step is through the mist to
the top of the fall.

But wilderness does not lie that close,
Steps to wilderness increase, as more people
reach out for solitude.

Continue—
if you are prepared.

 I got the allusions, all right. The Boy Scout motto, "be prepared," that was easy. And years of riding American roads was sufficient schooling for me to get a more "secret" message:

Prepare to Meet Thy God.

If I continued, the John Muir Trail would take me to a place where I would encounter a reality that lives the way a god lives. I had read the signs along the trail dimly, but now I understood them clearly. They were laid out to prepare me step by step to meet this reality face to face: the metaphor "heart of the world," the hint to leave the domestic self behind along with the dog, the exhortations to open the doors of all the senses, the use of science as scripture, the affirmation of faith in the interconnectedness of all things, and the appeal to separate myself from the many. I even remembered a sign I had passed by too quickly. It told me to look not just through the eyes of a geologist, or an artist, but also through the pupils of a child. Whoever wrote this sign had read the New Testament: "Suffer the little children. . . ." I imagined Ludlow's "King" opening the door of the Yosemite closet and whispering to me the name of his Kingdom: Wildness.

 I didn't continue along the trail. I heeded the sign. I wasn't prepared—not mentally, not spiritually, and certainly not to spend the night out. The mountains might ignite the spirit, but they have a tendency to leave the flesh cold. Thus, I joined the ranks of the many who venture only so far and then scurry back to the comforts of made-up beds and ready-made meals, not to mention already mixed drinks. As I walked downhill, I noticed how all the signs now had their backs to me. Implicit in their orientation was the message that I was going in the wrong direction.

It is now a decade later and the John Muir Trail I experienced is no more. I mean, the trail is there, but the interpretative signs along its initial leg from Happy Isles to Vernal Fall are mostly gone, except for those that warn of danger. They were put up in the early 1970s in order to make the park more user friendly after aggressive park ranger actions against the hippies, culminating in the riots in Stoneman Meadow in 1970, made Yosemite seem more prison than paradise. Posting the Muir Trail signs was, in a way, an evangelical move by the National Park Service to clue urban dwellers in on the secret that their salvation lay beyond the limits of the city. Interestingly enough, the signs also implied that the secret could no longer be found in the developed areas of Yosemite, which had, for all intents and purposes, become little cities. You would have to leave the valley with its comfortable amendments and take to the trails. Not only that, you would have to keep going on the trails, beyond the set stations where the many gather to gaze on standard Yosemite beauties.

*A Secret
at the Heart
of the Universe*

꩜

The signs were up not much more than a decade when the Park Service began taking them down. When I first noticed the early stages of their removal, on a hike in the mid-1980s, I was outraged. I went immediately to Leonard McKenzie, chief park interpreter at that time, to protest this sacrilege. He confirmed my suspicions. Yes, the signs were coming down and they wouldn't be put back. In reply to my indignant "Why?" he talked about scarring from public abuse and erosion from seasons of rain and ice. He also mentioned how a decade and a half had dated the message.

Despite my indignation, I understood his uneasiness. Some of the signs were disconcertingly corny. *Fragrant laurel leaves/Can you find them?* I imagined a kind old man in an official green suit speaking to people he thinks are nature illiterate. Even something like *What's that smell?* would have been better. Other signs seemed too dramatic, even a little hysterical, like *Stay on Trail/Stay Alive.* But, most of all, there was about the whole of them the sound of the pulpit. They preached. Whenever I read the signs aloud in class lectures, I noticed how my voice deepened to a sonorous, mock-sanctimonious tone. I could not help it. The students always laughed. Clearly, many of the hikers back in the 1970s and early 1980s had also laughed. So the Park Service got serious and took the signs down.

My sympathy for the Park Service's chagrin notwithstanding, I was still angry. Walking the trail from Happy Isles to Vernal Fall, paying attention to the natural world as the signs instructed me to do, had been profoundly satisfying, a religious experience of sorts. The testimony of the ages is that religious experiences are generally not available on demand. One needs a way, a path. That is why I was so interested in the John Muir Trail as it used to be, and why I felt so disappointed at the removal of the signs. The trail together with signs was both proclamation and path. It announced that the name of the secret that lies in the heart of Yosemite is Wildness. That its namesake was John Muir was most appropriate, for he had been from the late 1860s a prophetic voice crying "Wildness!" to the American people.

But the trail not only proclaimed. This route into the heart of light also provided access to Wildness. By following its path, pilgrims could arrive there both physically and spiritually. At its destination in the upper reaches of the High Sierra, they could find "the silent causes of power" and converse with the "King of all the Giants." Hiking the trail became, in effect, a sacramental act, a peripatetic ritual, a way of partaking of the power of Wildness. The signs along its initial stages served to initiate the hiker into the mysteries of Wildness, and so helped to formalize the ritual.

Wildness with a capital W. Typically, terms for deities are capitalized, as are some abstract nouns. Deity and abstraction are closely related in modern American religion. One hears "God is Love." God, here, is a personal, self-conscious being. One also hears "Love is God," by which is meant, presumably, that Love is the supreme algorithm of the universe, a procedure for solving the major problems of life. What about substituting "Wild" for "Love"? "God is Wild." Or, alternatively, "Wildness is God." Is that the credal summit that the John Muir Trail leads to? Is that the theological destination of the long and winding course of American thought about wild nature?

Ever since the advent of relativity and quantum mechanics, Americans under the influence of science have increasingly thought of the universe as an unimaginably colossal wilderness. While the world according to Newton was hardly a cozy neighborhood, it did seem fundamentally rational, well thought out and constructed, a continuation out there of the commonsense world we live in here. It was big all right, but not so big that we could not relate to it as our world. The universe according to Einstein, on the other hand, dwarfs the Newtonian, defies common sense, and contains the most mind-boggling of phenomena, such as quasars and black holes. It seems alien, inhospitable—the product and playground of utterly wild and incomprehensible powers.

One response to such threatening forces from without is to turn within and construct in our minds, our relationships, and our cities habitats of more humane proportions. Although these homes will finally be buried in a boundless graveyard (if the universe is an ever expanding one) or burned up in an all-consuming fireball (if the universe oscillates from bang to big bang), they are cozy enough for now. We can close the door on chaos and snuggle up close to our pet ideas.

This response is wholly understandable but only partially adequate. In particular, its dualism is disturbing. We must, I think, finally reject any human view that bisects a world that from all the available evidence is essentially whole. Splitting the world may not be as immediately catastrophic as splitting the atom, but the social and ecological consequences of dualism over historical time are just as destructive.

An alternative response is to reach out and embrace the wild forces of the universe and incorporate their spirit in our lives. Wild places on earth might be good locations for learning how to do this. Societies everywhere have spots in their cultural landscapes where ultimate reality, as they conceive it, is present in greater measure than elsewhere. The gods live in them, or have paid them a visit, or have designated them as somehow special. Holy places most intriguing to the imagination somehow embody in their very form and texture the shape of deity. Gothic cathedrals come immediately to mind. The God of medieval Christendom is high and lifted up, exalted beyond measure, and exceedingly holy. Hence, he is also, at times, cold and hard and hard to reach. The cathedrals dedicated to him express these same qualities in stone. They are made in his image.

Likewise, wild places embody the Einsteinian universe as no other terrestrial spots do. There cosmic forces are most obviously working out on earth their inevitable way. In this sense, wilderness is cosmic landscape. We in twentieth-century American society can go there to gain a meaningful rapport with the ground of our being. Or, in words that the makers of the John Muir Trail would have found more congenial, we can journey to Wilderness to hitch ourselves to a Wild Universe.

The phrase "God is Wild" makes sense, then, as long as we mean by "God" not a personal, self-conscious being, but the way the world works. "Wildness is God" says basically the same thing. By linking wildness with deity we are saying that wildness is for us a meaningful way to talk about the essential nature and function of the universe. We are also saying that this universal nature is manifested to us in a peculiarly powerful way in wilderness.

It is appropriate, therefore, to think of Yosemite's secret as a uniquely American "God" who lives way back in the wilder recesses of the American land, who can, in fact, be understood as the essence of that land. If we continue past the final sign on the John Muir Trail, past Vernal Fall and Nevada Fall into the High Sierra, and if we have prepared ourselves by opening ear, eye, nose, and mind, we will meet this deity and partake of its spirit. We will come to know Wildness.

No one I know who has made a pilgrimage along Yosemite's highway would claim full revelation. Ludlow is partly right, "Climb forever, and there is still an Inaccessible." Yet the Muir Trail attempts to transform what he took to be "Life's saddest lesson" into glad tidings: Yosemite discloses the "secret" in the heart of the universe, whose pulse can be heard beating in the rhythm of its rocks, rivers, and mountains, whose pulse can also beat in the veins of our interior landscapes.

In 1981 I turned back. The sign said, "Continue, if you are prepared." I was not prepared, so I did not continue. When David Forgang, curator of the Yosemite Museum, asked me to be park artist in residence for June 1994, I decided to get back on the trail. Not literally this time. I wanted to see if I could arrive in the heart of the wild by making a path out of words and photographs.

June 1, 1994   Merced River
I sit beside the Merced River opposite El Capitan. Left home a little after 8:00 this morning. Took four hours to get here. Spent most of the afternoon in photographic misdirection. Waiting now for evening shadows to fall across the river channel. The sky is clear, has been clear all day. Lots of azaleas around, a few bees and flies, no mosquitoes so far. Cars go by, entering the valley, the water from the Sierra Nevada and an ouzel travel in the opposite direction.

June 2   Below Vernal Fall
No wind. No clouds. Lots of people. No signs along the Muir Trail, except those announcing danger.

Camp Curry
Couldn't seem to get anywhere at Vernal Fall. So eating lunch here. A fussy Stellar's Jay just pooped on my black hat. At least he missed the nearby shake, though he couldn't have hurt it much. Getting a bit tired. Didn't sleep well last night. Went to bed at midnight and woke up at 5:00.

June 4   Yosemite Village
Leaning back against a Ponderosa outside of Degnan's. Sleptwalked through the morning. Trouble going to sleep. Trouble staying asleep.

June 7   Glacier Point

I can hear in the air the sound of Vernal and Nevada falls, like cosmic background noise.

June 9   Cascade Fall

Last night I went from room to room of a dream house looking for a way out of panic. I was not physically trapped. No way found. I remember saying, "What am I going to do? This is out of control." What I did was wake up.

This morning I posed in front of a white tuft of dead branches. The initial Polaroid print was pure white. "Must have left the shutter wide open," I thought. Did another one. Also pure white. Changed films. Also pure white. Put dark cloth over film holder to protect it from the sun. Again, pure white. Finally, I thought of the obvious, a major light leak. Sure enough, I had not secured the bag bellows.

The sun kept moving. I moved the tripod. I liked the composition. Exposure. A big dark blob was at the bottom of the print. The bag bellows was crumpled up between the front and back elements of the camera. Try again. I got in the picture and squeezed the bulb of the extension cable release. Nothing. No cliiick of the shutter for a one-second exposure. I had forgotten to cock it. Did so. On my way back to my spot in the composition, I got the extension cord entangled in small brush. This is panic!

Glacier Point

A small boy held on to the long arm of a large man. He was arriving. I was leaving. Our paths crossed on the concrete trail that connects Point with Parking Lot. Every few steps he would use the long arm for leverage and jump up in the air and shout, "Yippee! Yippee!"

June 10   Fern Spring

A small black car drives by. Slows as passenger leans out window and snapshoots. Car picks up speed.

Yosemite Falls

Three women, all in their fifties, probably, blonde to graying hair. They sit on a bench under a Black Oak on a hot, muggy, June Sierra day. One takes off a sock and strikes it against her bent knee.

June 11   Ahwahnee Hotel

I was racing someone. I started behind him. I said, "I guess there is no way for us to start even, is there?" Then we were off. I surprised myself in the dream, continuing to run hard even though making up no ground.

A Secret
at the Heart
of the Universe

🐚

June 13   Ahwahnee Hotel

I'm in the Ahwahnee parking lot, a middle-aged man leaning back against a middle-aged cedar. Sunny with high cirrus clouds. No wind.

   Last night at Happy Isles, under the dark cloth composing the Muir Trail, two crazy backpackers ran at the camera wildly.

June 14   Yosemite Village

A robin walked up to me. I talked to him. He made some sort of throaty noise. I asked him if he had a cough. I glanced up and a young boy, about four, was looking at me intently.

June 15   El Portal

Woke up repeatedly in the first hour of sleep; woke up repeatedly in the last hour. The night was an anthology of dramatic short dreams. I was always underground, or in a building, looking, searching, not so much for a way out.

   Confusion and misdirection. These past two weeks have been a wilderness of events. I have been wandering around in a wilderness of emotions. Is there a trail that leads somewhere? Probably not, no main trunk at least, just branches that branch again, forks that lack signs giving destination and distance. That this is so is no secret.

Heart Set on Yosemite #1. 1994. Polaroid Print.

Follow Your Bliss #4. 1994. Polaroid Print.

Signature of All Things #11. 1994. Polaroid Print.

Signature of All Things #20. 1994. Polaroid Print.

CLARENCE KING

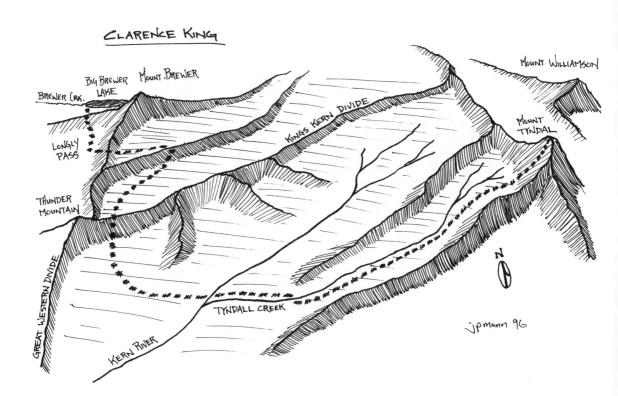

Mount Williamson

Mount Brewer

Big Brewer Lake

Brewer Crk.

Kings Kern Divide

Mount Tyndal

Longly Pass

Thunder Mountain

Great Western Divide

N

Tyndall Creek

Kern River

jpmann 96

CHAPTER TWO

Value in

Mountains

TRACKING CLARENCE KING
THROUGH SPACE AND TIME

The destination of the John Muir Trail is the summit of Mt. Whitney, the highest mountain in the contiguous forty-eight states. In 1864, a year after Fitz Hugh Ludlow found himself stymied at the foot of Nevada Fall, Clarence King set out to climb what he thought was the Sierra Nevada's highest peak. Bringing his hammer triumphantly down on its topmost rock, he named it Mt. Whitney. He soon realized, however, that a peak to the south was a helmeted head and shoulders taller than the one on which he stood. Apparently Brewer and the rest of the field party wanted the name of Whitney reserved for the highest Sierra mountain. So, after King's descent, they renamed the summit he scaled Mt. Tyndall after the English physicist and glacial geologist (King 1864; see O'Grady 1993, 116–17).

King had graduated in 1862 from Yale's recently founded Sheffield Scientific School and had set out the following year to make his geological fortune in the West. If he discovered gold dust and literary fame along the way, so much the better. Late that same year he found himself on a Sacramento River steamer with William Brewer, the right-hand man of Josiah D. Whitney of the California Geological Survey. Apparently the meeting was by chance, although with King's propensity to make fiction of his life, it is hard to be sure. He recognized Brewer, introduced himself, and promptly accepted an invitation to join the survey as Brewer's assistant.

The next year a field party under Brewer's leadership explored the western slopes of the southern Sierra in what is now Sequoia National Park. From a peak at the head of the Great Western Divide that the party named for their captain, King looked out over a vast expanse of granite, exposed as the downthrust of the Pacific plate uplifted the Sierra batholith. King looked. Ice-riven boulders everywhere littered the landscape. King kept looking. In the distance sharp spires cut the horizon. He desperately wanted to climb them. Eagerly he asked Brewer for permission to make a daring four-day forced march to what he thought was the high point along this crest. Permission was granted, reluctantly. He took Dick Cotter, the survey's packer, along with him.

From the slopes of Mt. Brewer, King and Cotter made their way over the Great Western Divide in the vicinity of Longley Pass. The initial night was spent on an icy ledge on the north side of the Kings-Kern Divide. In the morning they crossed this divide and descended into the huge amphitheater of the upper Kern River basin. Night two they camped in a grove of woods along Tyndall Creek, just east of the present route of the Muir Trail. The following day they determined to reach their destination.

As did early campaigners in Yosemite, King consistently used military metaphors for describing his mission to scale the pinnacle of the Sierra. He and Cotter had so far successfully scaled every battlement. Not far below the top of the mountain, however, it seemed that "Nature had intended to secure the summit from all assailants" and had "planned her defenses" with care, "for the smooth granite wall which rose above the snow-slope contin- ued, apparently, quite round the peak" (King 1872, 74). But King was not so easily deterred as Ludlow. He noticed that "quite near us the snow bridged across the crevice, and rose in a long point to the summit of the wall,—a great icicle column frozen in a niche of the bluff" (74). Cutting steps, the two men ascended the giant icicle until it became

> so thin that we did not dare to cut the footsteps deep enough to make them absolutely safe. There was a constant dread lest our ladder should break off. . . . At last, in order to prevent myself from falling over backwards, I was obliged to thrust my hand into the crack be- tween the ice and the wall, and the spire became so narrow that I could do this on both sides; so that the climb was made as upon a tree, cutting mere toe-holes and embracing the whole column of ice in my arms. (75)

After reaching the top of the wall and crawling out onto the smooth slope of granite that led to the summit, King turned around to watch Cotter.

He came steadily up, with no sense of nervousness, until he got to the narrow part of the ice, and here he stopped and looked up with a forlorn face to me; but as he climbed up over the edge the broad smile came back to his face, and he asked me if it had occurred to me that we had, by and by, to go down again. (75)

All that remained was an easy scramble along a narrow ridge to the apex of the mountain, which they reached, appropriately enough, at the apex of the day.

We had now an easy slope to the summit, and hurried up over rocks and ice, reaching the crest at exactly twelve o'clock. I rang my hammer upon the topmost rock; we grasped hands, and I reverently named the grand peak *Mount Tyndall*. (75)

What he actually said was "Mount Whitney."

King was of two minds in the Sierra Nevada. The great divides, like picket fences, seemed to spell "Keep Out" with letters made of cornices, crevices, and precipices. At the first sight of this message, he might have given up and turned back but for his other mind.

It would have disheartened us to gaze up the hard, sheer front of precipices, and search among splintered projections, crevices, shelves, and snow-patches for an inviting route, had we not been animated by a faith that the mountains could not defy us. (61–62)

It is not entirely clear what King's faith was in. Unquestionably, a not inconsiderable portion of his trust was deposited in himself. He and Cotter were "assailants" of mountain summits. They could outmaneuver nature's defenses with well-conceived and breathtakingly executed offensive moves. But his trust was also directed outward to the mountains themselves. Perhaps King's faith was similar to the American belief in capitalism, a confidence that the system as a whole, the operations of a market economy, will pay off for those who work hard enough. Analogously, he may have believed that mountains are part of a natural economy that rewards bravery.

August 7, 1989   Sunset Meadow

It is late in the evening. The drive down the San Joaquin Valley from Davis was hot, the detour by Cedar Grove crooked. We are doing a shuttle trip, in at Sunset Meadows in Sequoia National Park and out via Bubbs Creek in Kings Canyon National Park, so we left one car at Zumwalt Meadows. We parked the two remaining cars here and put our sleeping bags down in the dust. We are five, myself and four graduate students at the University of California, Davis. Sean O'Grady, who is writing a chapter of his dissertation on King, wants to walk in his footsteps 125 years later. Andrew Kirk, whose dissertation is on Shakespeare; Eric Paul Shaffer, whose dissertation is a literary biography of the West Coast poet Lew Welch; and Chris Ransick, a student in the creative writing program, have little interest in King. They are along for friendship.

August 10   Brewer Creek

Real weather happened for the first time today. I don't count the hail as we searched for a campsite on the ridge above Sugarloaf Valley on Monday, nor the rain as we climbed up from Roaring River along Avalanche Pass Trail on Tuesday. This evening, by a small lake near the headwaters of Brewer Creek, no hail came, no rain, but another kind of visitation. We arrived here about noon. Sean set off immediately to climb Mt. Brewer. I didn't have the stamina; I let him go on his bouldering way. Andrew and Chris trailed him as far as the saddle between Brewer and South Guard. Shaffer, as was his habit, jumped into lake.

I hauled Nikon and lightweight Gitzo up on a granite mound above the lake. The clouds came in fragments. Brewer covered and uncovered its head repeatedly throughout the cool afternoon. Now and then the westering sun lit up a ridge. I had a hard time piecing together a whole scene in the viewfinder, so I made several obligatory exposures and rockhopped down to a freeze-dried dinner.

After force-feeding chicken curry with falafels on the side, I meandered across little streams and pocket marshes out into the center of the basin. I thought maybe the sun, just before setting, might slip under the overcast on the western horizon and enlighten the world around me. I soon realized that the scene I had previsual- ized was not going to happen. In my mind I had fast-forwarded the sun to a small clearing in the western sky and imagined it turning a brilliant red beam on the curls of smoke hanging from the sky above me. In real time, when the sun reached this clearing, it was already occupied by a dark, dense bank of clouds.

Just about the time I finished taking camera off tripod, and tripod off its perch on a nearly level granite boulder, I noticed something big coming from the west. It was a huge cloudcraft, round, grey, soft, moving slowly, even deliberately, up Brewer Creek. Hovering close above the granite floor, it just fit the basin and set- tled in. A cold, moist precipitant out of the universal atmosphere came coolly to rest around me. Because it took up all my space and occupied my entire vision, it seemed, in fact, to be the universe.

August 11   North of Kings-Kern Divide
We are completely enclosed by high granite peaks and spires. To the west is the Great Western Divide, which we crossed via Longley Pass. To the south lies the Kings-Kern Divide, which we hope to cross tomorrow. Sloping gradually off in the direction of Lake Reflection is a series of spurs to the north, each an abutment to Mt. Brewer or one of its attendant peaks. To the east is Mt. Jordan, a peak offset to the main line of the Kings-Kern Divide. Each cold promontory has con- densed its own cloud above it, and airy wisps trail over all the ridges. A lot of thunder rolls around the basins, but little rain has fallen.

Late this afternoon, sunlight did manage to slip in underneath the cloud cover, indicating that out in the San Joaquin Valley all was clear. At first, pale pink and then bright orange clouds surrounded us on all sides. The orange was so deep that I suspected forest fires still ran in the Sierra foothills to the west. I turned all about to take in the panorama. Then, gradually, I settled down into a calmer, more medita- tive emotion as the colors faded into shades of grey: the brown-grey of the granite merged with the blue-grey of the fog brushing the ridges, while the cumulus clouds above provided an off-white highlight. This space between day and night seemed to remember the one and anticipate the other, as late autumn, after the deciduous col-

ors have faded, remembers summer and anticipates winter. A fulcrum, this here and now, this moment balanced between white and black, this calm.

August 12   South of Kings-Kern Divide

It's just before sunset, on this the third day of weather. We are camped beside the largest lake in the canyon that leads from the Kern River to Thunder Pass. Diamox is making the bones in my fingers buzz. The mosquitoes are also buzzing. All of us are rather quiet, probably because of the recent proximity of danger. Crossing Thunder Pass, which took us over the Kings-Kern Divide, was hardly death defying. Yet the presence of snow and ice on the upper slopes turned a mountaineering-book class two into a genuine fourth-class struggle.

Now, after dinner, we are letting our emotions down, step by step. I sit facing west, looking at the junction of the two great divides. A level, dark mass of cloud lies over a buttress of the Kings-Kern crest. It looks like a gigantic hooded figure whose draped arms are spread out to the east and west. To me it is the resident spirit of this place, pronouncing benediction upon all our ascending and descending. Another cloud shape, a long streamer, runs from the crest of the Great Western Divide to a spot right over our heads. Its orange is so luminous I wonder if the color is courtesy of Frederick Church.

Quickly the orange is gone, though not the mosquitoes, and I hear the zip of tents being closed against them. The sky has become a study in late afternoon grey. The moisture in the air, like a diffusion filter, has softened the mountain edges. Large, dark masses of condensed air drape the peaks and fan out over the granite ridges with their cold, deep gashes. Above are light-grey clumps with middle-grey wisps trailing beneath. This is the time of day my black-and-white eyes like the best, as they scan the tonal scale from light to dark, resting finally on the ominous but irresistibly black crevasses.

The next day the weather passed on, leaving us to walk across the upper Kern Basin under a vast dome of blue. We passed the grove of trees on Tyndall Creek where King and Cotter had slept and set up our tents at a small lake off the trail to Shepherd's Pass. The following day O'Grady and I climbed Mt. Tyndall. King described his route so clearly in *Mountaineering in the Sierra Nevada* that it was no trick at all to repeat it. I didn't go to the top—some crazy notion of intentionally stopping just short. But from a perch just below it, I saw what he had seen a century and a quarter before.

That day in 1864 was like this one in 1989: cloudless, the sun a white point on a blue background, the earth radiating light. I have always considered King's description of a no-weather day in the Sierra the most accurate ever written.

> The serene sky is grave with nocturnal darkness. The earth blinds you
> with its light. That fair contrast we love in lower lands between bright
> heavens and dark cool earth here reverses itself with terrible energy.
> You look up into an infinite vault, unveiled by clouds, empty and
> dark, from which no brightness seems to ray, an expanse with no
> graded perspective, no tremble, no vapory mobility, only the vast
> yawning of hollow space. (78)

The last word, "space," is the decisive clue for understanding King's experience in the Sierra Nevada. He looked around and saw no movement: of sun, of clouds, of life. He listened and heard no noise: of bird, of mammal, of human. Since we know time by the stop and go of motion and by the rise and fall of sound, for King on Mt. Tyndall, time was not. Yet space radiated out dramatically in all directions, including up and down. Above, it was "hollow." Below it was full, though the forms were motionless and silent. The contrast between the presence of space and the absence of time induced in him an emotion he had never felt before, an inner calm to match the still without.

> I thoroughly enjoyed the silence, which, gratefully contrasting with
> the surrounding tumult of form, conveyed to me a new sentiment. I
> have lain and listened through the heavy calm of a tropical voyage,
> hour after hour, longing for a sound; and in desert nights the dead

stillness has many a time awakened me from sleep. For moments, too, in my forest life, the groves made absolutely no breath of movement; but there is around these summits the soundlessness of a vacuum. The sea stillness is that of sleep. The desert of death, this silence is like the waveless calm of space. (80)

King's description reminded me of the Sierra experiences of John Muir a few years later. Both men had spatial imaginations. From a boyhood in Scotland, an adolescence in Wisconsin, and an industrial accident in Indiana that left him temporarily blind but permanently determined to forsake the mechanical for the natural, Muir arrived in California in 1868 and briefly visited the Sierra Nevada. He returned for the summer of 1869 to accompany the flocks of San Joaquin rancher Pat Delaney on their seasonal migration from the Central Valley to Tuolumne Meadows. He revised the journal he kept that summer and published it as *My First Summer in the Sierra*. The clear, blue, expansive Sierra days caught his attention again and again, but his response was far different from King's. The cloudless heavens, instead of being nocturnally grave and empty, stretched their arms over him in loving embrace. Nor did the landscape blind him with its terrible light. Instead, it "beam[ed] with consciousness like the face of a god" (85).

If the landscape is facial, then its various features should make a unified countenance. In other words, it ought to be intelligible. Muir found it to be so on the top of Mt. Ritter three years after his first summer and eight years after King climbed Mt. Tyndall. From the summit of Ritter he studied the view in all four directions, much as King did. He felt sympathy for the "inexperienced observer," who is often "oppressed" by the view "from an all-embracing standpoint" because the jumble of mountain peaks, glaciers, rivers, and meadows seems so "incomprehensible." But once such scenes are studied "one by one, long and lovingly," and especially in the light of glacial action, the "far-reaching harmonies become manifest. . . . Then, penetrate the wilderness where you may, the main telling features to which all the topography is subordinate are quickly perceived, and the most ungovernable Alp-clusters stand revealed, regularly fashioned, and grouped like works of art" (Muir 1911a, 68–69). "Revealed," says Muir, as a god might reveal itself. Through science, in this case the science of geology, God's design was uncovered, and so Muir came down from the heights of Ritter reassured that even the apparently chaotic world of the High Sierra made sense.

My experience in 1989 was quite different from King's and Muir's. It was more an experience of Time than of Space. I witnessed the temporal delight with which the universe condenses itself out of clear air and then evaporates. I liked best the grey moments after the glory and before the darkness, and so found myself drawn more to the somber King than the cheerful Muir. The twilight seemed to acknowledge my presence in the universe and immediately call it into question. My place in space was brief in Time, like the evening itself. My time in the mountains was also brief. After the descent from Mt. Tyndall, we crossed Forester Pass and followed Bubbs Creek back to two apple pies à la mode.

Time + Space = the Einsteinian Universe. One value in mountains is the opportunity it allows for us to situate ourselves in the universe as we understand it and to accept the emotional benefits of knowing our place. King and Muir reached out and fastened their clamps to the extension of the universe. I hitched myself to its duration. The emotional results were pretty much the same in all three cases. For King on top of Mt. Tyndall, space was "waveless"—a vacuum, hollow, empty, still. He was calm, therefore. On top of Mt. Ritter, space was an inhabitory consciousness for Muir—a presence, godlike, intelligible, even loving. He was calm, therefore. For me, at the juncture of the great Sierra divides, time was the coming of evening storms, and their going. I, too, therefore, was calm.

Gary Snyder came from Kitkitdizze, his home on San Juan Ridge in the northern Sierra Nevada. With him were another resident of the Ridge, Paul Noel, and Tom Lyon, a professor at Utah State University in Logan and editor of *Western American Literature*. I brought with me a longtime friend, Hal Faulkner (who more than anyone else taught me how to use a 4x5 view camera), and three colleagues from the Davis campus of the University of California: Professor of Education Vince Crockenberg, microbiologist Mark Wheelis, and toxicologist Bruce Hammond. It was October 3, 1986. We gathered on the Sierra Nevada's sharp eastern side to celebrate thirty-one years later the climb of Matterhorn Peak by three Dharma Bums: Snyder, Jack Kerouac, and John Montgomery. Montgomery was well known only inside of Beat Generation circles. I never met him, although before his death we exchanged several letters about his Matterhorn climb with Snyder and Kerouac and about his efforts to persuade his employer, the U.S. Post Office, to issue a special Yosemite stamp in 1990 to mark its centennial as a national park.

The Davis five arrived in Bridgeport at one-thirty. We had lunch in the Sportsman's Inn, where the Dharma threesome ate after their climb in 1955. I ordered a grilled cheese sandwich, chips, and Coke, my usual junk food before a hike in the mountains. The meal was mediocre, but for dessert I led an expedition across the street to the local bakery and the tastiest fruit bars in the state. We then cruised the sidewalks, checked out the Mono County shining white courthouse and peered through the windows of the closed Mono County Museum until Snyder, Noel, and Lyon arrived at three.

We left the Twin Lakes trailhead a couple of hours later, crossed Horse Creek, and took a broad path along the lake. At the point where it forked, Snyder thought we should head up. I thought we should continue on the level, even though a sign announcing the need for a wilderness permit was posted up the hill. I felt sure that I had taken the lower route back in the spring of 1985, the only other time I had been in the area. Confidently, I led straight ahead. After several hundred yards, however, the path did not gradually begin the ascent I thought it should. We got out the topo map and, sure enough, the trail not taken was the right one. We turned around, and now I was the tail.

Over a thousand vertical feet later, where the trail from Cattle Canyon intersected Horse Creek Trail, we discussed stopping. Wheelis and Snyder, both of whom had been up Matterhorn before, knew that not many good camping places lay ahead. But we decided to push on, wishing to make the climb the next day as short as possible. After another mile, where the trail disappears in a maze of shrubbery, Wheelis, Hammond, and Snyder went ahead to hunt for a site. While they were gone, Lyon found a mostly level clearing down the hill by the creek. We called the others back and set up camp.

Snyder located a cozy bivouac under the trunk of a tree that had fallen over but had been caught by another tree before it hit the ground. It provided excellent protection from dew and was snow free. After a lengthy survey of the area I finally decided to put my sleeping bag out in the open, in a small snowfield, where it would be soft. Not a smart move, as I should have known from adopting the same strategy on Mt. Shasta the previous spring. Feet that stick out beyond the end of the foam pad melt the snow, and sleeping bags that wrap those feet absorb cold along with the moisture. Ten toes go numb.

While eating dinner we stood around the fire and talked. Snyder reminisced about his trip with Kerouac and Montgomery. He confirmed what I had thought: that Kerouac's narrative in *Dharma Bums* was basically accurate, though fictionalized to make Snyder (Japhy Ryder in the book) more heroic and Kerouac (Ray Smith) less brave than was actually the case. Kerouac had liked the idea of rucksacks because he did a lot of hitchhiking and train hopping. He had seen how Philip Whalen and Snyder used them, so Snyder gave him one for a present. Then one night Snyder and Montgomery pulled him out of some bar in San Francisco and headed up over Sonora Pass. They got all the way up into Horse Creek Canyon before he "woke up." "It's so quiet," he said. "What's going on?" He didn't realize he had been taken out of the city until all was still. Snyder confessed that the trip was the product of Jack's craziness multiplied by his own.

I fell asleep rather quickly for me but then woke up about midnight. I had no watch and so estimated the time by the position of the stars and by the gauge in my bladder. Much of the remainder of the night I spent awake, toes getting ever colder, and watched those two uncanny creatures, Taurus and Orion, trek across the night.

We started up Horse Canyon about eight, after my favorite backpack breakfast of Swiss muesli and bagels loaded with cream cheese and black-berry jelly. More appropriately in light of what lay ahead, Snyder had gruel with nuts. Soon we were strung out: Lyon way out in front (in my next life I want a wiry body like his); Crockenberg, Wheelis, and Hammond an ath-letic threesome; then a more rickety threesome of Faulkner, Snyder, and me. Noel brought up a distant rear. I was happy to have him along.

Snyder stopped often to take notes. Partly he was trying to recreate his route with Kerouac. He pointed out the big rock where the 1955 party had spent the night. In addition, he transcribed the tracks in the snow, measur-ing them with his pencil. I found out later his surmises: two bear cubs play-ing some distance from mother, two coyotes that had preceded us over the pass, a badger, and lots of deer. Seeing him take notes made me wish I had brought my notebook along. I comforted myself with my standard line: I too was taking notes, but with silver instead of lead.

The first mile was up a steep glacial cirque. At the top of it Lyon and the other front-runners waited for the rest of us. The next section was fairly level, across Horse Creek and through small shrubs—easy walking. Then we began to climb more steeply up the right side of the canyon. Noel at this point said he was holding us back and was surely not going to make it to the top. Maybe he would try to reach the pass and look over into Yosemite, but we were to go on ahead. Actually, once freed from responsibility, he kept the pace remarkably well until lunch, which we ate just below the pass.

At the head of the pass was a marvelously well preserved terminal moraine, about a quarter of a mile long and maybe fifty feet high. The area immedi-ately above it had been scooped out with remarkable symmetry by the glac-ier, which had melted down to a broad snowfield. We crossed into Yosemite National Park, looked down into rockbound Spiller Canyon, and peered up at Matterhorn, our first view of it since leaving camp. From back there the very top arete had been visible, beautifully lit by yesterday's evening sun. We had been walking for hours today, and still it seemed a long way off. It was a long way up. We had more than a thousand feet left to go.

I was already exhausted. Getting sick, too. Like I was hungry without wanting anything to eat. I tried to nurse along Coffee Nips for stimulus and energy but found them more and more disagreeable. In desperation I began to count steps. I figured that I was proceeding upward at about nine inches per step, minus a three-inch slide in the sand back toward the sea. We were led by the indefatigable Lyon straight up the scree slope, about half covered with snow, which gave firmer footing than the gravel. I calculated that it would take me two thousand steps to reach the top.

So I started to count. Ten, twenty, thirty. The idea was to walk fifty steps before stopping; that way I could pace myself. But it didn't work. I could take no more than twenty-nine steps before having to stop, gasping for breath. Lyon and Crockenberg quickly became a faraway twosome; Wheelis, Hammond, Faulkner, and Snyder in the middle, in that order; and me, the caboose, now that Noel had turned back. And losing ground. At step 1,200 things improved. I now knew that my stomach was going to hold on. But I had to pick up the pace, for it was after two.

At the foot of a third-class scramble of some fifty feet, still about a hundred feet from the summit, I came upon Faulkner. The exposure had gotten to him. He said he was pulling a Kerouac:

> I now began to be afraid to go any higher from sheer fear of being too high. I began to be afraid of being blown away by the wind. All the nightmares I'd ever had about falling off mountains and precipitous buildings ran through my head in perfect clarity. . . . I looked back and like Lot's wife that did it. . . . *"This is too high!"* I yelled. I was really scared. . . . Finally I came to a kind of ledge where I could sit at a level angle instead of having to cling not to slip, and I nudged my whole body inside the ledge just to hold me there tight, so the

wind would not dislodge me, and I looked down and around and I had had it. *"I'm stayin here!"* I yelled to Japhy. (Kerouac 1958, 82–83)

Faulkner showed me the direction the others took, and off I went. I like feet-over-hands climbing and so moved with more agility than I had all day. At the top of this cliff I came out on a jagged shelf, maybe six feet wide, and looked virtually straight down the other side. My stomach bounced against my throat. It was the moment that mountain climbing is made for. In another two minutes I was on the summit with the others. 1828, 1829, 1830. There. One hundred and seventy steps under estimate. Snyder had arrived only fifteen minutes ahead of me.

I greeted everyone with a shake of hands, male style, and began taking pictures. It was a struggle. I was thinking like a muddy, meandering river while all about were the jagged edges of glacier-carved granite. Yet I couldn't afford to rest. It was already three-fifteen and the sun would set at six-thirty. We had five miles and four thousand feet to go down. No way was I going to make it back to camp before dark. Kind for kind, as I snapped the shutter, Snyder composed this poem:

> On Climbing the Sierra
> Matterhorn again
> after Thirty-one
> years
>
> Range after range of
> mountains
> year after year after year
> I am still in love
>
> (Snyder 1992a)

Too soon we gathered our gear and began the descent. I had been on the summit crag for a quarter of an hour. On the third-class part of the descent,

I was too unsteady for comfort and once almost tipped over. Hands shook as cupped fingers searched for cracks and feet groped for ledges. Wheelis guided me down past the most difficult section. I had counted on being able to glissade down the snowfields, gaining time and saving energy, but they were too mushy. Next I tried a run, jump, and slide on the gravel, but the boulders were too big and my knees too weak. I settled reluctantly on taking each step at a time. I envied Kerouac his descent. Clinging to the side of the mountain, he had heard Snyder on top give out "a beautiful broken yodel of a strange musical and mystical intensity" and then,

> suddenly everything was just like jazz: it happened in one insane second or so: I looked up and saw Japhy *running down the mountain* in huge twenty-foot leaps, running, leaping, landing with a great drive of his booted heels, bouncing five feet or so, running, then taking another long crazy yelling yodelaying sail down the sides of the world and in that flash I realized *it's impossible to fall off mountains you fool* and with a yodel of my own I suddenly got up and began running down the mountain after him doing exactly the same huge leaps, the same fantastic runs and jumps. . . . With one of my greatest leaps and loudest screams of joy I came flying right down to the edge of the lake and dug my sneakered heels into the mud and just fell sitting there, glad. . . . I took off my sneakers and poured out a couple of buckets of lava dust and said "Ah Japhy you taught me the final lesson of them all, you can't fall off a mountain." (Kerouac 1958, 85–86)

It wasn't funny how my mind foreshortened the distance home. I expected to see camp a full two miles before it actually came into view, still a disgustingly long way off. By this time I was slurring every third word. I could speak coherently only by collecting the sentence and mouthing it word by word. Wheelis stayed with me as I fell a mile or more behind the leaders. By the time I reached camp, there was barely enough light left to avoid the cross-country trees. A fire was going, and Snyder had fixed me some tea. After a few

sips, I dragged my sleeping bag over next to the people. I felt like a kid, wanting to be close. I was not hungry, nor even tired anymore. An empty calm settled into stomach and bones. I lay down and listened. Snyder proposed a
round of toasts. One to me, the organizer. I smiled to myself in the darkness.
One to Kerouac. "A great writer though not as appreciated as he ought to
be." "To Jack," all said, and I thought my yes in silence.

Muir on the side of Mt. Ritter back in 1872 got himself in a situation like
Kerouac's. It was late in the season. It was late in the day. He pushed on, all
the while telling himself to turn back. Almost to the summit, high above the
saddle between Mt. Ritter and Banner Peak, he found himself holding on
to the mountain.

> After gaining a point about half-way to the top, I was suddenly
> brought to a dead stop, with arms outspread, clinging close to the
> face of the rock, unable to move hand or foot either up or down. My
> doom appeared fixed. I *must* fall. There would be a moment of bewil-
> derment, and then a lifeless rumble down the one general precipice
> to the glacier below. (1911a, 64)

Then came his "rescue":

> When this final danger flashed in upon me, I became nerve-shaken for
> the first time since setting foot on the mountain, and my mind seemed
> to fill with a stifling smoke. But this terrible eclipse lasted only a mo-
> ment, when life blazed forth again with preternatural clearness. I seemed
> suddenly to become possessed of a new sense. The other self, by-gone
> experiences, Instinct, or Guardian Angel—call it what you will—came
> forward and assumed control. Then my trembling muscles became firm
> again, every rift and flaw in the rock was seen as through a microscope,
> and my limbs moved with a positiveness and precision with which I
> seemed to have nothing at all to do. Had I been borne aloft upon wings,
> my deliverance could not have been more complete. (64–65)

TRACKING MOSES ON HIS WAY TO SINAI

Origins. Ancestors. Ancestors of King, Kerouac, and Muir. In a former life I was a scholar of the Bible. In this present one, the magnets of modern languages have hopelessly scrambled the file containing Greek, and Screen-Saver is relentlessly deleting Hebrew word by word from my consciousness. But I still teach courses on the Bible as literature and occasionally write an article or two on those old sages Job and Qoheleth. So, when it is a question of beginnings, I can't help it, my mind always selects *The Bible* from the menu of possibilities.

Moses. While shepherding the flocks of his Midianite father-in-law on the slopes of Mt. Sinai, Moses encountered a deity whom he had not previously met. He knew a divine being was present because a bush was not turning to ash, even though it was on fire. The figure in the plant introduced himself as none other than the God of Moses's forefathers—Abraham, Isaac, and Jacob—and then commissioned Moses to go back to Egypt and help his kinspeople escape the rule of Pharaoh. Once beyond the borders of Egypt they were to return to Mt. Sinai and worship him. Sinai was not, however, to be their ultimate destination. The Israelites were eventually to arrive in Canaan, a land abundant with milk and honey. Moses knew better than to return to his people in Egypt and tell them a No Name God wanted their allegiance. So he asked for and got the personal name of the God of Abraham. It was Yahweh.

Later, after a divinely engineered escape from Egypt, Moses led the Israelites to Sinai, just as he had been told to do. Several stops were made along the way. When they arrived at Marah after three days of dry camping, only bitter water was available to drink (Exodus 15:22–25). At Rephidim they had no water at all (Exodus 17:1–7), while just before that, in the Desert of Sin, they had had no food to eat (Exodus 16). The Israelites complained again and again to Moses about their hunger and thirst. In Egypt Pharaoh had served slavery along with a full platter. Moses in the desert dished out freedom on an empty plate. They thought maybe the former condition was preferable. Moses had saved them to kill them.

Again and again Moses responded. He said, in effect, "Your anger is not really directed at me, but at Yahweh. In objecting to his care of you, you are putting him to the test. You doubt that he will provide for you. But he will, as I am about to show you. Once I demonstrate how capable he is, it will be your turn. Yahweh wants to see if you will rely on him. You will pass the test by following his orders."

Yahweh easily passed the care test. He sweetened the water at Marah (Exodus 15:25). In the Desert of Sin he provided meat in the form of quail and bread in the form of manna (Exodus 16:13–14). At Rephidim he made water come out of solid rock (Exodus 17:5–6). The people, on the other hand, demonstrated a remarkable facility for flunking Yahweh's examinations. To be sure, they obeyed sometimes; more often they did not, or did not for long. They were almost perverse in disregarding Yahweh's instructions for the collection and storage of manna, and at each new crisis they renewed their complaints, as if they had learned nothing from the previous one.

The idea of wilderness as a place where testing occurs should sound familiar to American ears. Constantly I hear it from the mouths of backpackers and mountain climbers. What seems to be tested in these modern situations, however, is not deity (or that which exists at the order of magnitude of deity) but personal prowess and courage. For us, the individual is placed in the crucible of wilderness and examined for strength and durability. The doctrine and practice of self-help picks up the rhetoric of American capitalism and transports it to the high country. From rags to riches by hard work becomes from slope to summit by self-reliance. To pass the test of stamina, one must dig way down deep inside and find what it takes to get to the top. This is the way that Clarence King thought. He was an exemplary American athlete.

King's feats of derring-do are impressive. Nevertheless, up to a very important point, I have a preference for the biblical way of construing the basic issue. In Exodus, an order that exists beyond the self is put to the test.

The essential question is, What about that order? Is it reliable? Once evidence of its reliability is brought forward, a response is called for. The narratives leave no doubt that the proper response is reliance.

Faith is a good English word to use in naming this act of reliance. I mean by *faith* what I think Christians mean, if we focus on form: committed action based on trust in what one believes is trustworthy. The difference between us has to do not with the nature of the behavior, but with the object of the preposition *in* when we say, "faith in _____." This brings me back to the qualification expressed in the previous paragraph, "up to a very important point." Moses asked the Israelites to place their faith in a being beyond the natural world. This meant that they could survive in the wilderness without having to learn its ways. Yahweh could be counted on to poke his hand in from outside nature and supernaturally provision a whole company of his followers marching through an arid land. If wilderness is a trope for the natural world as a whole, and I use it that way, then the stories in Exodus tend to imply that human beings can live faithfully in the world without having to pay it any mind.

Still, the Bible need not be thrown out with the supernatural bathwater. The stories of Moses on the way to Sinai do a good job of posing an important question: Are we spiritually sufficient unto ourselves, or is wholeness to be found only in relation to the whole? They also give, formally speaking, what I believe is the right answer: Health is in the whole, and the medicine is faith.

A moment of clarity allowed John Muir to climb up Mt. Ritter. Sudden enlightenment allowed Kerouac to cavort down Matterhorn Peak. *Satori* is possibly a good word to use in describing the experiences of both men as they clung to the sides of two of the Sierra Nevada's most famous mountains: the one ascended and the other descended Zen-style. But I find Zen-talk exotic. *Satori* is not in my native vocabulary. *Faith* is. Curiously, the only one of the foursome—Moses, Muir, King, and Kerouac—to actually use the word *faith* is the one whose understanding of it was the most limited. Hanging on a Sierra precipice, King reported that he and Cotter were "animated by a *faith* that the mountains could not defy us" (1872, 62, emphasis added). It seems fair to say that King's trust was mostly in himself. Nature's function was to reassure him that his self-confidence was not misplaced.

The faith of both Muir and Kerouac, on the other hand, was fundamentally in the mountains themselves, when mountains are the local manifestation of the everlasting procedure of the universe. Mountains are valuable because they put us in the position of faith or unfaith. They so place us in the four dimensions of this world that decision making is hard to delay, much less avoid. Muir and Kerouac responded out of some intuitive realization that, however scary the world, squeezing themselves snugly into tight crevices was not the faithful move. Trust was the proper attitude, and to "sail down the sides of the world" was the appropriate activity.

On the sides of Matterhorn Peak, at the angle of unrepose, Kerouac had learned the final lesson: the universe will sustain you without striving on your part. I did not feel that I learned anything so cosmic. I came close to falling, not off the mountain, of course, but nevertheless down. I leapt not down the side of Matter but lead-footed it back to camp. I could hardly talk, much less shout. But in my bag, by the fire, with friends, released from reaching by exhaustion, I was, for one of the few times in my goal-grasping life, simply there. I slept eleven hours, without waking, without dreaming.

Value in

Mountains

PHOTOGRAPHIC RECLIMB

Late in the summer of 1993 I organized a reclimb of Matterhorn to collect words and pictures. I knew I would never make it carrying camera as well as backpack, so I enticed three of my friends not only to go along but to carry some of my equipment. They were Sean O'Grady (the same Sean who had organized the climb of Mt. Tyndall) and two different graduate students in the Department of English at the University of California, Davis: Katrina Schimmoeller and Chris Sindt. I even paid them, but not close to what they were worth.

September 18, 1993   Spiller Canyon
Cold. I am cold. Sitting back to rock; it's about eight, after dinner. Directly in front of me is Matterhorn, about 1,400 feet up. My feet are stuck in sleeping bag. Over bag is Sean's bivy sack. I have on long-legged underwear, then heavy sweat pants, short-sleeve shirt, long-sleeve shirt, sweatshirt, down jacket. And I'm cold.

Bad day photographing. Hurried. Harried. "Slow down," I said, and promptly kicked one leg of my tripod out of place. Then hit the top of my head on overhanging granite. Had to sit down and laugh.

September 19   Spiller Canyon
Just back from top of Matterhorn. Knees hurt with every step, despite many Ibuprofen. Trina carried tripod most of way up and most of way down. Chris carried backpack down last 500 vertical feet. Way up was easy for 30 minutes. Then wind hit. A constant blowing through the body, pore by pore, knocking hat off, making it impossible to think. No good photographs. The descent was emotional letdown. Jet flying over with other realities on board.

September 20   Horse Canyon
Sitting on ground, early night, back to log at the rock where Kerouac and Snyder slept in '55. Sean has a great fire going up against the already blackened granite.

We play around with the camera, composing our cooking gear into a still life. Yesterday was struggle. Today ease. Just as I stuck head out of sleeping bag this morning, clouds were a soft pink over the summit of Matterhorn. After breakfast, I went up about 400 feet onto the side of the mountain. Had a wonderful time photographing. I called one series "You can't fall off mountains" and another "The closer you get to real Matterhorn."

Getting too dark to write, but I don't want to turn flashlight on. Sometimes it is better not to see. Water of Horse Creek runs down to Twin Lakes and out Walker River to evaporation in basin and range territory. Elemental night air returns to Sierra lodgepole forest. Stars go by on the circumference of the largest circle we know. Four human animals go up canyon and over a pass piled with fractured rock, spend two nights, climb a mountain, and go the other direction down. They sit by a fire and talk easily, not about great things, kidding each other, having hopes.

Matterhorn Peak #1. 1993. Polaroid Print.

The Closer You Get to Real Matterhorn #1. 1993. Polaroid Print.

You Can't Fall Off Mountains #10. 1993. Polaroid Print.

You Can't Fall Off Mountains #6. 1993. Polaroid Print.

Mesa Trail

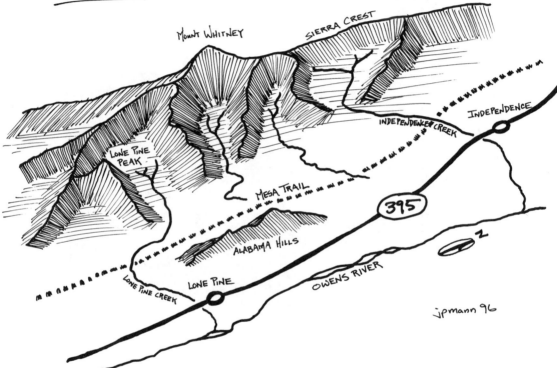

Mount Whitney

Sierra Crest

Independence

Independence Creek

Lone Pine Peak

Mesa Trail

395

Alabama Hills

Lone Pine Creek

Lone Pine

Owens River

jpmann 96

CHAPTER THREE

Lost

Borders

THE MESA TRAIL

January 6, 1994   Death Valley

On the way to Dante's View, I noticed how much taller were the creosote bushes beside the road. Not only taller by maybe a third, but fuller. Why? Instantly I turned scientist. Hypothesis One: Disturbance of soil from highway construction. Hypothesis Two: The plants by the road had no competition on the highway side. Hypothesis Three: Runoff of water from the pavement. I voted Number Three the most plausible. Surely the creosote bushes along the right-of-way flourish because they get more water. They must be pleased. I am a little like them. My roots drink up words that run off literary roads. I, too, am pleased.

The Mesa Trail begins at the edge of town. Actually, there are two towns, one of them native, the other exotic. The trailhead is a partially fenced field that Indians and sheep used to frequent. From there you walk, or preferably let a horse do the walking, since the distance is great. You go south, orienting yourself by a prominent peak in a massively raised mountain range. You keep the range on your right side and the river that runs parallel to it on your left, not going up into the mountains nor down to the river. Hold more or less a level course. In fifteen miles or so you will go past some strange-looking hills, like bubbles protruding from the plain. Another few miles will bring you to a big, salty lake. You continue, past the lake, and into a land that seems to have no orientation and no borders.

If the time is about 1900, one town is Independence. The other town is a long-established Paiute Indian settlement beside Pine Creek. If you want an expert guide, you can stop by "the brown house under the willow-tree" (Austin 1903, xi) on the west side of Independence to see if Mary Austin is available. She calls the trailhead Naboth's Field, the peak Oppapago, and the lake Bitter. Twilight Hills is her label for the peculiar rocks. Sometimes she refers to your destination as Shoshone Land. Mostly, however, because she has "a great liking for the Indian fashion" (vii) of naming a place by what it is to the one who does the naming, she calls it "the Country of Lost Borders" (3).

If the time is near the year 2000, Independence is still Independence, but the Indian town is no more, replaced by a row of RVs stationed at Independence Creek (not Pine Creek) Campground. A few grinding holes mark the site of the former village. The Eastern California Museum and its asphalt parking lot now own and occupy Naboth's Field. U.S. Highway 395 runs a little below the Mesa Trail and parallel to it. The Anglo designation "Lone Pine Peak" has replaced the Indian name "Oppapago," and modern maps label the hills "Alabama" and the lake "Owens." South and east of the lake are the precise and known borders of China Lake Naval Weapons Center and Fort Irwin Military Reservation. Farther south is Twenty-Nine Palms Marine Corps Base. Farther east, a long way farther, is Las Vegas.

Mary Austin is no longer available, but her books are, if, six decades after her death, you still are interested in the "Land of Lost Borders" and want help in finding it. Two of them are particularly helpful: *The Land of Little Rain* and *Lost Borders.* You can pick up the Mesa Trail in *The Land of Little Rain,* at the start of the chapter with that title.

> The Mesa Trail begins in the campoodie at the corner of Naboth's
> field, though one may drop into it from the wood road toward the
> canyon, or from any of the cattle paths that go up along the stream-
> side; a clean, pale, smooth-trodden way between spiny shrubs, com-
> fortably wide for a horse or an Indian. It begins, I say, at the
> campoodie, and goes on toward the twilight hills and the borders of
> Shoshone Land. It strikes diagonally across the foot of the hill-slope
> from the field until it reaches the larkspur level, and holds south along
> the front of Oppapago, having the high ranges to the right and the
> foothills and the great Bitter Lake below it on the left. The mesa
> holds very level here, cut across at intervals by the deep washes of
> dwindling streams, and its treeless spaces uncramp the soul. (143–44)

The Mesa Trail is the line on the map of western America where real path and spiritual way meet and become one. It begins at the edge of limitation, which is, at the same time, on the outskirts of the real Euro-American town of Independence and the real Native American village on Pine Creek. The route goes in the physical direction of south past familiar landmarks, and simultaneously, takes the traveller into uncharted territory. It ends up in an actual desert of many enclosed basins, which is also where borders are lost. There, in the dry hills, where "there is room enough and time enough," is desert heaven, where "Trees grow to consummate domes; every plant has its perfect work. Noxious weeds such as come up thickly in crowded fields do not flourish in the free spaces" (87–88). In the "free air and the free spaces of Shoshone Land" (101), your soul can "uncramp" (144). You will lose your bearings but know where you are.

February 16, 1991   Bishop
The coast down Sherwin Grade towards the Land of Lost Borders is one of the world's great rides. Today I sat back and smiled in fifth gear. Rolled down the window and banged the palm of my hand on top of the Honda. Boundary Peak was off to the left. Soon left it behind.

By population and by volume, the principal people on the Mesa Trail are animals and plants. Most prominent are the shrubs; "social," Austin calls them, because they appear to have allotted ample space to each other, as if "by election." All remain content within their "purlieus," each allowing its woody neighbors plenty of branch room, and each cultivating under its "stout twig[s]" its own "clientele" of flowers, "larkspur in the *coleogyne,* and for every spinosa the purpling coils of phacelia" (144–45).

Evening Snow (*Linanthus dichotomus*) Austin especially liked, because children named it, and "it is no use trying to improve on children's names for wild flowers" (146), and because of its adaptation to desert heat. From the height of a horse at midday, you look down into an empty space, only to discover that once the Sierra Nevada has shaded the declining sun, the ground is covered with "snow." Once, in the late afternoon, I spotted the very white flowers of this plant. I knelt down, opened Peterson's *Field Guide to Pacific States Wildflowers* and searched until I discovered its common name. I returned to the very same spot the following day, only to spend a quarter hour in the hot sunlight before I located it.

The "late slant light of the mesa" (149) also brings out the burrowing owls, who are so in place in the desert that their call seems the very color of evening breaking into sound: "If the fine vibrations which are the golden-violet glow of spring twilights were to tremble into sound, it would be just that mellow double note breaking along the blossom-tops" (149). The night belongs to the predators—red fox and, Austin's favorite, the coyote, who "goes garrulously through the dark in twenty keys at once, gossip, warning, and abuse" (150). There are always prey and, usually, leftovers for scavengers like the buzzards, who "mak[e] a merry-go-round" in the perfumed air (153). Austin knows that badger, though "no sportsman" (151), sometimes comes up out of the burrow empty-mouthed, and that expectant crows do not inevitably find already chewed carrion. All in all, however, her deepest conviction is that flora and fauna on the Mesa Trail fit with each other and fit in with the limits set by soil and weather.

Austin's deepest wish, unstated but clear, is that the human animal were likewise so well adapted. Back in the first chapter, she gives explicit expression to this desire.

> The desert floras shame us with their cheerful adaptations to the seasonal limitations. Their whole duty is to flower and fruit, and they do it hardly, or with tropical luxuriance, as the rain admits. It is recorded in the report of the Death Valley expedition that after a year of abundant rains, on the Colorado desert was found a specimen of Amaranthus ten feet high. A year later the same species in the same place matured in the drought at four inches. One hopes the land may breed like qualities in her human offspring. (6–7)

She believes that the land has been successful with at least three human genera: Indians, vaqueros, and shepherds. All three of these groups "have their season on the mesa" (156). She is content to describe them in general terms, with only one individual mentioned by name, Petite Pete, the shepherd. With him the chapter on the Mesa Trail comes to an end. But not the trail.

SATURATED WITH THE ELEMENTS

February 17, 1991   Big Pine
Big Pine Motel, Room 14, late at night. This afternoon I stopped at Baker
Creek Campground. At the edge of the road was a concrete camera, about five
feet by three feet. It was maybe a foot thick. A big hole in the center served as
an aperture and a short section of corrugated pipe as a wide-angle lens set on
infinity. Seemed as if I could release the shutter of unbounded desire.

What "The Mesa Trail" lacks in specificity in its description of desert humans, Austin makes up in the stories she tells about her three heroes, who
have their own separate chapters: the Pocket Hunter, Winnenap the
Shoshone, and Seyavi the Basket Maker. All three of them are, in a sense, on
the Mesa Trail. For example, each of them is, in a fundamental way, alone.
"A pocket," Austin explains, "is a small body of rich ore occurring by itself"
(66). So, too, the Pocket Hunter, is rich in desert know-how and almost always by himself. Because Winnenap was a Shoshone among Paiutes, having
once long ago been offered as hostage, he also lived to himself, although he
married into the tribe and was a respected doctor. He lived, as did his fellow
Shoshone, "like their trees, with great spaces between" (88).

The death of Seyavi's husband in a battle with white men left her alone
with her young child. She distilled her experience in managing personal
dislocation and tribal displacement into baskets and into a proverb: "A man
must have a woman, but a woman who has a child will do very well" (163).
Because Austin herself felt emotionally abandoned by her husband, and because she considered herself a weaver of words, Seyavi is clearly her favorite
character. That her own child was mentally retarded, a condition she did
not recognize at first, made her situation, from her own point of view, just
as desperate as the Basket Maker's. Although Seyavi lived in an Indian village, Austin always treats her in her aloneness. "This was that Seyavi who
reared a man by her own hand, her own wit, and none other," she says.
Since Seyavi had to "win sustenance from the raw material of life without

intervention," she did not have "the sleek look of the women whom the social organization conspires to nourish" (176).

All three of these characters accommodated themselves in remarkable ways to the conditions of the land. Seyavi, like the reeds that went into her baskets, "lived next to the earth and w[as] saturated with the same elements" (169). The Pocket Hunter was so "saturated with the elements" (70) that he had the capacity "of taking on the protective color of his surroundings" (43). Therefore, "he came to no harm in it; the land tolerated him as it might a gopher" (68).

We might say that Winnenap's accommodation was to culture rather than land. He acquiesced in his role as hostage. He accepted the role of doctor when it fell to him, as well as the conditions of employment. But Austin, at least with regard to native inhabitants, makes no distinction between culture and land. Indian culture in the desert is like coyote culture or creosote culture. The "wisdom of the tribe," in a culture so long adapted to little rain, is the same as the wisdom of the land. And so, when three of Winnenap's patients die in the midst of an epidemic of pneumonia, he, too, has to die that the "force of the disease" might be "broken" (100).

The Pocket Hunter, Winnenap, and Seyavi act with a curiously intentional nonintentionality. "Born with the facult[ies]" of pocket hunter and doctor and artist (66), they seem to be as genetically adapted to a habitat of little rain as the coyote is. Yet, also like the coyote, they give the impression of going about their business deliberately. They accept what is given, but not passively, not stoically, not with resignation. One suspects that it is their ability to act—not so much within limits, but with limits—that Austin admires so much. Limits are their partners for life. As a result, their lives have an elemental quality, like the Pocket Hunter's kitchen:

The simplicity of his kitchen arrangements was elemental. A pot for beans, a coffee-pot, a frying-pan, a tin to mix bread in—he fed the burros in this when there was need—with these he had been half round our western world and back. He explained to me very early in our acquaintance what was good to take to the hills for food: nothing sticky, for that "dirtied the pots;" nothing with "juice" to it, for that would not pack to advantage; and nothing likely to ferment. (64–65)

An elemental kitchen makes for a simple but wholesome diet. An elemental life "uncramps the soul" (144) and permits a "communion of the stars," which in the desert "look large and near and palpitant; as if they moved on some stately service not needful to declare" (21). These travellers on the Mesa Trail feel that they are "in the grip of an All-wisdom that killed men or spared them as seemed for their good," but never subjects them to ignominious deaths. "Of death by sickness [the Pocket Hunter] knew nothing except that he believed he should never suffer it" (71).

January 2, 1994   Bishop

I turned the Honda off 395 onto a narrow lane on the north side of town. A late afternoon winter sun lit up the cottonwoods in the pastures nearby and the White Mountains behind them. Drove east past two women and a man who were picking up downed limbs out in the fields. Drove another half mile to generate the courage to ask them about going over the fence. Turned around and came back. "Is it all right to hop the fence and walk around in there?" I asked through the open car window. "Oh," one of them said, "all this is public land. You can go anywhere you like. And you don't have to climb over the fence. There are turnstiles all along and even gates like the one over there. Just make sure you put the wire back over the post so the cows don't get out."

All of sudden I could go where I thought I couldn't. Surely this is the way to put up fences, if we must have them. Build them with rickety, unlocked gates and turnstiles here and there. So we can get over and out.

The Pocket Hunter wanders away from civilization. Winnenap lives on the edge of his adopted tribe. Seyavi is sufficient unto herself. We have no trouble believing that they are travellers on the Mesa Trail. The mythology of the American West and the journey of quest in cultures worldwide prepare us to accept these "loners" as trailblazers. The hero with a thousand faces has the support of the community but goes it alone. We will misread Austin, however, unless we realize that for her, people who live in community can also take the Mesa Trail. The complements of Winnenap, Seyavi, and the Pocket Hunter in *The Land of Little Rain* are the towns of Jimville and El Pueblo de Las Uvas.

Of course, it is true that Jimville is not just anytown situated anywhere convenient. Austin spends nearly two pages commenting on the difficulty of getting to it and, once there, of getting out: "It is said of Jimville that getting away from it is such a piece of work that it encourages permanence in the population" (106). In Jimville it is as if a thousand Pocket Hunters settled down without losing their hardy adaptation to the desert. Because "there [was] not much intervention of crops, cities, clothes, and manners between [them] and the organizing forces to cut off communication," they understood "the language of the hills" (120). How much noise you allow between yourself and the elements, that is what determines whether you are on your way to the Country of Lost Borders. Reduce the static and you can hear what the land says. Listen to the land and you walk the Mesa Trail. Maybe alone. Maybe together.

> The hills say, "Of all [our] inhabitants [we have] the least concern for man" (68).
> The hills say, "[There is about us] an elemental violence" (109).
> The hills say, "It is all one, there is gold enough, time enough, and men enough to come after you" (119–20).

The hills say, "Life, its performance, cessation, is no new thing to gape and wonder at" (121).

Listening to the hills, the people of Jimville become neither "embittered" nor "mean-spirited." Instead they respond with "a certain indifference, blankness, emptiness if you will, of all vaporings, no bubbling of the pot . . . no bread-envy, no brother-fervor." There is something "pure Greek" about their philosophy of life, in that they have "the courage to sheer [*sic*] off what is not worth while." They "endure without sniveling, renounce without self-pity." They "fear no death" and "rate [themselves] not too great in the scheme of things" (121). There is about them and inside of them "the repose of the perfectly accepted instinct" (121). This is Austin's most succinct description of the spirit-state of her heroes. The desert is as it is. The coyote and the crow come with instincts adapted to it. So do her heroes. When conditions (of the land) match instincts (of the living), repose of body-mind results.

The Little Town of the Grape Vines is the opposite but equal of Jimville. The list of opposites is long: gentle for its rough, soft against its hard, little villainy instead of "killing and drunkenness" (120), a garden in place of bare ground. The language spoken is "A purer Castilian than obtains in like villages of Mexico" (280), not English. September 16 is more important than July 4. The visits twice yearly of Father Shannon are occasions of great solemnity. Surely a stare would be the only salute he would get in Jimville.

Yet the two towns are equal to each other in deep philosophy. Both take death as part of life. Neither is obsessed with its own importance. The populations of both are connected to the land. They are "earthborn" (279) and their buildings are "a piece of earth" (280). Work, at least in the Protestant sense, is the measure of neither woman nor man. Jesus Romero gives up his job for his family:

I go to the Marionette, I work, I eat meat—pie—frijoles—good, ver' good. I come home sad'day nigh' I see my fam'ly. I play lil' game poker with the boys, have lil' drink wine, my money all gone. My fam'ly have no money, nothing eat. All time I work at mine, I eat, good, ver' good grub. I think sorry for my fam'ly. No, no, señora, I no work no more that Marionette, I stay with my fam'ly. (270)

Not surprisingly, then, the end mental result is the same for the inhabitants of both towns: the "ease" (281) of Las Uvas just matches the "repose" (121) of Jimville.

February 21, 1991   Lone Pine

Dream #1. We were watching a movie. Ellen was there, and Jeannette and her
mother. We all left the theater together and walked on a road. Then Ellen veered
off, strangely, as if onto a freeway ramp, but still walking. When I realized she
was not with us, I waved to her. She seemed to be going in the right direction.

   Dream #2. Karen was trying to break a horse. It was in a large open space, so
she had to make an enclosure with bales of hay. She did not succeed.

   Dream #3. I was trying to get U.S. emigration papers for a Mexican woman
and her family. She was trapped by being a Mexican in the U.S. without papers.
The papers would free her.

The walking woman, the hero of Austin's final story in Lost Borders, is
the quintessential Mesa traveller. She makes for herself a xeric way in the
desert; the desert makes for her a xerothermic self.

> She was the Walking Woman, and no one knew her name, but be-
> cause she was a sort of whom men speak respectfully, they called her
> to her face Mrs. Walker, and she answered to it if she was so inclined.
> She came and went about our western world on no discoverable er-
> rand. . . . She came and went, oftenest in a kind of muse of travel
> which the untrammelled space begets, or at rare intervals flooding
> wondrously with talk, never of herself, but of things she had known
> and seen. (196)

She went into and came out of the desert like a mirage. Had she "some
place of refuge where she lay by in the interim" (196)? No one knew. Did
she limp? Many thought so, but consider the distance she covers. Was she
sane? Most thought not, yet "in her talk there was both wisdom and information" (199). Have men molested her? No, everybody agreed to that, even
though she slept over at herders' camps and laid over for weeks at one-man

stations. It was puzzling. Most women stayed out of trouble in a land beyond the limits of the law by making their behavior "ladylike" (198). It was decidedly not ladylike "to go about on your own feet, with a blanket and a black bag and almost no money in your purse, in and about the haunts of rude and solitary men" (198). Yet Mrs. Walker got no affront.

The narrator first heard of her at Temblor, then again at Carrisal, and for a third time at the Eighteen-Mile House. They met several times at ranch houses and road stations, but those places permitted only the exchange of pleasantries. Finally, at Warm Spring in the Little Antelope the two women were alone with each other, and their talk "flow[ed] as smoothly as the rivers of mirage through the blue hot desert morning" (200). Their talk came round to children. Upon learning that her companion had had one, the narrator admitted that "it was one of the perquisites of living [she] should be least willing to do without" (201). The Walking Woman responded that "there were three things which if you had known you could cut out all the rest, and they were good any way you got them, but best if, as in her case, they were related to and grew each one out of the others" (201).

The narrator then lets the Walking Woman tell "her case" in the first person. She worked with a man, not for, not beside, but as one person in two bodies. That was the first thing. They saved the flock in a violent desert storm. Afterward, she was no more tired than the earth was. Nor was he. They made love. That was the second thing.

> "To work together, to love together," said the Walking Woman. . . .
> "There you have two of the things; the other you know."
>   "The mouth at the breast," said I.
>   "The lips and the hands," said the Walking Woman. "The little, pushing hands and the small cry." There ensued a pause of fullest understanding, while the land before us swam in the noon, and a dove in the oaks behind the spring began to call. A little red fox came out of the hills and lapped delicately at the pool. (207)

The lovers remained together through the summer. The baby came in October. She did not know "if she would have given up her walking to keep at home and tend him," but "the baby had not stayed long enough for that. 'And whenever the wind blows in the night,' said the Walking Woman, 'I wake and wonder if he is well covered'" (208).

From the narrator's point of view, the Walking Woman had learned what there is to be learned on the Mesa Trail. "She had walked off all sense of society-made values, and, knowing the best when the best came to her, was able to take it. Work—as I believed; love—as the Walking Woman had proved it; a child—as you subscribe to it. But look you: it was the naked thing the Walking Woman grasped" (208–9). The two women parted.

Far down the dim, hot valley I could see the Walking Woman with her blanket and black bag over her shoulder. She had a queer, sidelong gait, as if in fact she had a twist all through her.

Recollecting suddenly that people called her lame, I ran down to the open place below the spring where she had passed. There in the bare, hot sand the track of her two feet bore evenly and white. (209)

The Walking Woman had an invalid to care for that left her "broken in body." After her (or perhaps his) death, came "other worrying affairs," and on top of them, an indefinite illness. The narrator muses, "It might very well have been an unsoundness of mind which drove her to the open, sobered and healed at last by the large soundness of nature" (199). Here is Austin's credo. There is a soundness in nature, a soundness that is capable of healing human unsoundness. Walking is a course of healing, a way to let nature's medicine work.

It is not easy to describe what Austin means by "the soundness of nature." She never explicitly says what it is. She shows it in action. She presents us with people healing and healed. Better tell stories than talk abstract philosophy. Yes, true, I do not disagree. But I also think it is possible for us, on the basis of her stories, to draw some general conclusions about her meaning. Theologians of the Middle Ages found it less difficult to say what the Christian God was not than to say what it was. Following them down the Via Negativa may be a good way to start.

Most obviously, Austin does not mean by "the soundness of nature" that a special power inhabits nature while also transcending it, a power that is capable of straightening its switchbacks for human convenience. Nor does she mean that nature is in the process of implementing some sort of universal plan. Teleology does not grow in the desert. "The soundness of nature" does not mean, for Austin, that nature pays special attention to human beings. Whatever sort of system the universe is, it does not alter its operations for the benefit of humans, alone or in aggregate. She does not mean by "the soundness of nature" that the universe behaves morally, or that it is morally intelligible. To speak of good or bad deeds, that she is willing to do; she will not say that nature is good or bad.

Within these parameters of "is not," can we say what for Austin the soundness of nature is? Possibly. Perhaps. Yes, cautiously. Austin seems to mean by "the soundness of nature" that the earth is good habitat for humans. It is good habitat for *Homo sapiens sapiens,* just as it is for *Canis latrans* and *Atriplex confertifolia.* Just as it once was for *Pterodactylus* and *Tyrannosaurus.* At some time in the indefinite future it will be habitable no longer. In the meantime, the habitat is small, minuscule in relation to the size of the whole, but sufficient. There is food for us here, enough to nourish the entire person in all of its body-mind-spirit complexity. No need exists to jump planet, before or after death, no need to return at a later date.

The soundness of nature is the naked thing that the Walking Woman seizes. She is, therefore, free. Austin promises us nothing less, if only we will get on the Mesa Trail and pursue it to the end. Freedom is the destination. It is not, however, a freedom outside of limits. It is not abandon. Deeply embedded in American culture is the image of lonely, socially alienated souls, walking out past society's limits to places where they can do exactly as they choose, as if all things were possible. The Walking Woman may look, at first, as if she were one of these people. She is not. To be sure, the trail she walks ends up in "the Country of Lost Borders." What happens there, however, is not the loss of limits, but an exchange of one maker of limits for another. There, "not the law, but the land sets the limit" (1903, 3). The land sets the limit; its inhabitants, therefore, are free. The land of the free is where "the manner of the country makes the usage of life" (88).

Austin agrees with just about all other philosophically minded people who have thought about freedom: it is possible only within constraints. Bondage is constraint by human-made conventions. Freedom is constraint by the conventions of the universe. Nature is sound because its conventions will, if followed, promote human freedom. And the end result of freedom gained and practiced is a "repose of the perfectly accepted instinct" (121). The Walking Woman got that far, as did Seyavi, Winnenap, and the Pocket Hunter, and not only them, but the inhabitants of Jimville as well, and those of El Pueblo de las Uvas.

Sometime in 1990   *Kitkitdizze*

Carole Koda said   *An Orange-Crowned Warbler sang in the Black Oak yester-*
day. Every repeat was full and strong. No "the world is too
full of warblers anyway." No "why keep this up, no mate is
coming or ever will."

Gary Snyder said   *This is Zen. To give a hundred percent and know it does not*
matter.

I have often wondered what course the environmental movement might have taken if Mary Austin, instead of John Muir, had been adopted as eponymous ancestor. It might not have survived infancy, for Austin's sympathies are too broad. Adversarial organizations need adversaries. It is hard to find them in Austin. Granted, she is not shy about taking an occasional jab at readers she considers too comfortable, and here and there are characters with few, if any, redeeming qualities. But basically her policy is inclusion. Indigenous Americans and Immigrant Americans, miners and ranchers and farmers, people alone, people together, all manner of vegetation, from *coleogyne* to creosote bush, all manner of animation, from buzzards to burrowing owls, all of biology is included. Not that all are equal, of course. She has her favorites, such as Indians and coyotes, while rabbits are a bit too "foolish" (25) and sheep too destructive. Yet even the sheep, environmental enemies Number One to Muir, her arms enclose.

If not then, what about now? The American nature-oriented community, as it exists today, might profit from giving her books more than a speed read. The lone male on a long march into the wilderness would not be ruled out of order. He would, however, be asked always to consider the large soundness in nature. The wilderness might become more living space than refuge. Community might become not the source of disease, but group living in place. The rapid pace of feet going to work or to the wild might slow to a saunter. Walking might become the practice of choice. Relationship to the whole might become the goal. A deeper repose might be the result.

March 31, 1994   Independence

Yesterday, I was snapping Polaroids on the southern edge of town, looking down the Mesa Trail toward Oppapago. Kids from a nearby house came out. Two girls about ten, one smaller than the other. One boy, very funny, maybe a little older. The two girls were "best friends." One was from Las Vegas, staying with her grandparents while "Mom" went to school. They wanted to know what I was doing. Seems like the whole school had seen this strange man all in black with a big camera wandering around town. Speculation was rampant. Now the three of them had the chance to scoop their classmates.

> *"Are you writing something?"*
>
> *"Yes."*
>
> *"Are you famous?"*
>
> *"No."*

They were all energy, especially the girls. I began putting them in the pictures. Soon I just let them make up the poses. We had a great time.

> *"Will we be famous from these photographs?"*
>
> *"No."*

I gave each one a print. They insisted that I sign them and write down a title. I couldn't think of a title. I hesitated. Then I wrote my name. I wanted to write something like, "On the Mesa Trail." But I knew I wasn't on it. At best I was beside it, in the runoff ditch.

Oppapago. 1994. Polaroid Print.

Mary Austin's Home #2. 1994. Polaroid Print.

Lost Borders. 1994. Polaroid Print.

The Mesa Trail #4. 1994. Polaroid Print.

THE LONELIEST ROAD

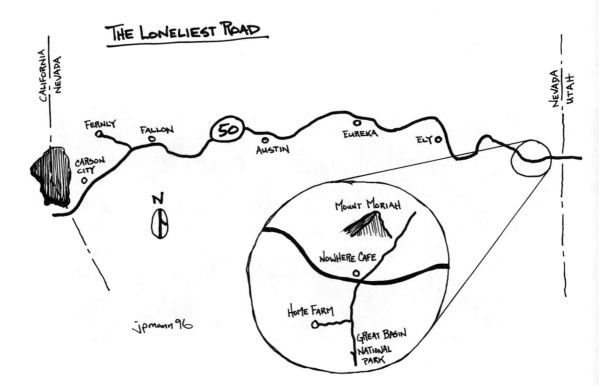

CALIFORNIA / NEVADA

FERNLY

FALLON

CARSON CITY

50

AUSTIN

EUREKA

ELY

N

NEVADA / UTAH

MOUNT MORIAH

NOWHERE CAFE

HOME FARM

GREAT BASIN NATIONAL PARK

jpmann 96

The Loneliest Road in America

THE ROAD

It begins at the Nevada-California line. At the Nevada-Utah line it ends. Both beginning and ending are arbitrary. They were established by boundary commissions for reasons that have nothing to do with logical places to start or conclude a journey. This trip is a game.

"Nevada State Line," announces a small sign above a traffic light. It is superfluous. Two huge monsters sit on either side of the street, one named Harvey, the other Harrah. With skins of glass, flashing eyes, and mouths of many doors, they signal that the gaming has begun.

At first, the road is broad and paved. It runs east through luxurious *resortia*, and then turns north along the east shore of a pool of cool water collected by a *graben* of geological proportions. It follows the billboard course of human events: Horizon Casino Resort, Love's Lake Tahoe Wedding Chapel, Family Medicine and Urgent Care, Nuggets, Slots, Fantasy Girls, Topless Cabaret Nightly, and a Free Six-Pack of Coke. Sam's Place has it all: food, spirits, and sport.

January 15, 1994   Nevada Beach
Ate lunch here. The park was closed for the winter, so we left the car by the road barrier and walked down. In a large sandy field of picnic tables and Jeffrey pines ate tuna salad on crackers and chocolate chip cookies. A jogger trotted by, beaming with the virtue of locomotion under his own steam. Nearby yellow pines composed a scene of lake and mountain so purely blue that even the snow took the dye. Jeannette asks, abruptly, "Do you travel because you want to get somewhere?"

After tunneling through a rocky knee, the road makes a right turn east again and curves up out of the Truckee watershed. Only trees are present now, mostly yellow pine, some cedar, no homes. Over Spooner Summit the highway goes and then swings down through sweeping turns into the valley.

The pines thin for thirst; ceanothus and manzanita scrubs fatten on aridity. On the distant plain, Sierra water channeled by the Carson River moves slowly through Carson Valley on its way to Carson Sink.

March 11, 1994   On the Road
Driving along the shore of Lake Tahoe. It's a pleasant day. 40 degrees. Low
clouds hanging over the mountains. Willows blush red in the creek beds. No wind
at Zephyr Cove Resort. Fences around the houses at Skyland, and a gate to go
through to get in. Over Spooner Summit I go, elevation 7,146. Brake Check
Area. Then a pullout, where a monument tells of a big fire in 1926. Five
firefighters were killed, all of them prisoners at the time. Governor Scrugham is-
sued full pardons so they could be buried as free men. Runaway Truck Ramp.
Down into the Carson Valley, fifth gear, foot off accelerator, coasting. Last Run-
away Truck Ramp.

Highway 50 is an exercise in how to be free. Will it be gaming, spirits, or sports? What about taking a trip? Make the start arbitrary. Pretend I have no past. Make the finish arbitrary. Pretend I have no future. I am just on the road.

Carson City is the place to come for food, fuel, and vehicle. Highway 50, as it enters town from the west, is a broad avenue of bright and shiny auto dealers, discount stores, and fast-food chains. Wal-Mart, McDonald's, Mervyn's, and Supply One. Buick/Oldsmobile, Ford/Mercury, and Toyota at a single intersection. Nissan down the road a block. A mile of miraculous American (and Japanese) manufacture. If money is a problem, there is always the other side of town, the domain of cars previously used.

At the far eastern end of town is a junkyard of cars previously wrecked. That is not a good ending. Neither is the free plot those firefighters purchased with their lives. Better to get in my car and keep going, past Carson City. If, in my eagerness to escape both past and future, I go too fast, I can always hope for a runaway person ramp.

April 25, 1994   Carson City

I am sitting at a big table in Rich Moreno's office doing the scholarly thing of going through folders he has collected of Loneliest Road materials. It's about 1:30 in the afternoon of a spring storm. Rich is on the phone raising money while I'm reading newspaper articles, stacks of them, about an advertising coup. Life *said, back in 1986, Highway 50 across Nevada is the "Loneliest Road in America." Don't take it, they advised, unless your "survival skills" are honed. How ignorant of the cult of American character can you get! A higher recommendation of Highway 50 to Americans like myself, who quest for solitude, could hardly be imagined.*

Rich Moreno was more wise. Rich was a student at Davis back in the late 1970s, early 1980s. We've been thumbing back through old UCD times. He worked for the Nevada Commission on Tourism when the article in Life *appeared and is now publisher of* Nevada Magazine. *He and fellow commissioner Roger King knew that if we solitary pilgrims got the news that Highway 50 was lonely, we'd be there, so many of us so soon that it wouldn't be lonely for long. So they got up this ad campaign, with a feature story they sent to hundreds of newspapers. They issued "Survival Kits" and posted "Loneliest Road" signs along the way from Fernley to Ely. Eureka labeled itself the Loneliest Town, and Churchill County Museum put out a sign on the outskirts of Fallon declaring that it was the Loneliest Museum of them all. They even provided a Loneliest Telephone. Thus did Highway 50 in Nevada become the Vision-Quest Route through the Outback of late-twentieth-century America.*

Nevadans cannot seem to make up their minds about fences. Along its entire length Highway 50 is liberally provisioned with signs that display a spirited longhorn bull, tail swishing, and the words "Open Range." Many people, I bet, choose to live here because it is "Open Range," a place where they intend to maximize their individuality and minimize interference from troublesome neighbors and meddlesome government. And yet, they make some ambiguous statements about freedom with the way they fence their property.

Not far east of Carson City is Carson Plains, a typical Nevada "suburb." It runs along the highway for several miles and crawls up onto the flanks of the hills to the north, a mile or two away, a sizable development. On the western end is a planned subdivision, just like one would find at the edge of any growing American city: houses, all of them minor variations on a theme, shoved up next to each other along curving streets. Everywhere else the lots are large and uniform, squares on graph paper distributed evenly between the asphalt lines. Most squares contain homes, and most of these are "mobile," although they have not moved in years. A few squares are vacant.

Carson Plains is unincorporated and far enough away from urban conformity that people can presumably do what they like with their yards. Along Frontage Road are three mobile homes in a row. Around the first two are no fences. The third sits between two identical stretches of wire fence on the east and west; the property is open to the south and north. Clearly these fences are markers only: a public declaration that here is where you end and I begin. They are not meant to keep anyone out. Yet, three more squares to the west is a veritable fort! It, too, is "mobile," sitting on a raised platform of dirt. Around it huge boulders have been bulldozed into place, making access impossible except through a narrow driveway. In the middle of the front yard is an underground bunker, the Nevada equivalent of the castle keep.

Scattered across the Carson Plains are examples of every gradation imaginable between "no fence" and "fort." Wooden fences and frail wire fences.

Sturdy wire fences and barbed wire fences. A house on Lafond Road says it all. The owners have completely cleared the ground around the edges of their property but erected no fence. In the middle sits a white clapboard house with a green watered lawn in front of it. Around this core area runs a barbed wire fence. On the driveway gate are two flat cardboard figures, bent over as if they are tending a garden, with oversize buttocks turned toward the passerby. One figure says, "Private Drive." The other, "No Trespassing."

The question Carson Plains raises in all but words is what to make of fenced-in things. The problem is this: What keeps alien *out* may also keep occupant *in*. Not physically; the issue here is one of spirit. Fear may be the motivation for keeping others out, and fear may cause us to fence ourselves in, even though we tell ourselves that the fences are purely defensive. It is possible that what we really fear is ourselves. Along Highway 50 are four other fences. Two of them surround prisons, one between Carson City and Fallon and the other east of Ely. Two others make compounds out of Lazy B and Salt Wells, the state-supervised brothels east of Fallon, strategically placed to attract customers from the Fallon Naval Air Station. These fences put limits on two forms of excess: criminality and sexual license. Are we saying by the fences we erect around our private property that we, too, need to be contained? They could be signs that we are afraid not only of what other people might do to us, but also of our own impulses for gratification and, perhaps, for retaliation.

Clearly, freedom is both attractive and scary. No fences opens up the territory of self-realization. "Open Range," the signs say. But no borders may also mean no limits. Maybe we will go too far out there, beyond our ability to set limits for ourselves. Some sort of fence may be needed, even if mostly symbolic. Nevada has plenty of models to choose from.

From Fallon to the Utah border is a multimillion-year-old Nature Park built by colliding plates and stretching continent. The Ride is Up and Down and the Theme is Basin and Range. Out of the Carson Sink and into Dixie Valley, where Navy jets from Fallon go war gaming. Around the south end of Clan Alpine Mountains, then parallel with them to New Pass Summit in the Desatoyas. Across the plain of the Reese River to Austin. Over in quick succession Austin Summit and Scott Summit and a little later Hickison Summit. Fast along a straight shot of almost twenty-five miles and up into Eureka. Over Pinto Summit and down. Over Pancake Summit and down. Over Little Antelope Summit and down into White Sage Valley. Over Robinson Summit and into Ely. Southeast in Steptoe Valley to get over the Schell Creek Range. A turn northeast to get through the Snake Range. Down one more time to the Utah border.

All of the summits are densely populated with piñon pines and junipers. Even from the seat of a passing car, a passenger can distinguish the yellow-green junipers from the more grey-green piñons. On the descents the piñons thin, until there are none. The junipers, more tolerant of heat and aridity, continue down the ridges and scatter about over the rolling foothills. None make it into the flats below. Looking ahead, drivers can always chart their vertical course. The sequence of mixed-green forest to yellow-green woodland to grey-brown chaparral means a falling altimeter. Even one lone juniper visible from the salt flats is a sign of ascent.

Human debris along the highway means a town is coming. The more the debris, the bigger the town: trailers unattached with all tires flat, pickups abandoned to weather, dilapidated farmhouses bereft of people, decaying signs of businesses probably defunct. East of Fallon there are only three: Austin, Eureka, and Ely, almost evenly spaced. In most mountainous regions of the world, towns and cities are at the base of the hills, beside the rivers, spreading out into the plain. Carson City fits the worldwide model.

But in the middle of Nevada, along Highway 50, while mountain ranges are many, rivers with water in them are few.

Instead of rivers, central Nevada has mines. The mines are in the mountains, so that is where the towns are, either huddled atop ridges, like Austin and Eureka, or tucked into canyons, like Ely. What this means for the winter traveller is cold during the day and colder at night, with a freezing wind night or day. Winter is just the right season for these towns, which have exchanged the heat of precious metals for cooler tourist coins.

March 11, 1994   On the Road
On Eight-Mile Flat of salt heading toward Austin. It's dusk now. Light grey, soft lens clouds, a little pale blue showing through. The land light brown, mountains in the distance snow covered. After two cars pass in the opposite direction, nobody's on the road but me. I like this time of day. Land darkening into nearsightedness, the sky turning off by rheostat. Headlights on bright.

"It used to be called Y Cafe, because the intersection of 487 with 50 made a Y. Customers would walk in and say, 'This is the middle of nowhere!' So, we decided to call it that. *Nowhere Cafe.* Our son made the sign out there. Lots of people stop and take a picture of it, but you're the first one with that big a camera."

Ellen Hyde grew up on a farm about five miles from Baker, still a little town despite the fact that it is now the "gateway" to Great Basin National Park. She has watched the decades of the twentieth century bring some minor changes, like paved roads and electricity, and a few more travellers.

"Otherwise not much has changed," she said.

"True," I thought. It looked as if generations of *Artemisia* still called most of the land home, giving way not to encroaching suburbs, even of the Nevada type, but only to junipers and pinons as the Snake Range coiled itself into Wheeler Peak.

Ellen had a stroke in 1979, three years after she and her husband, Kenneth, bought the cafe. They sold it soon after that and moved to Oregon, only to have to repossess it in 1985. "It was not open, then open, then not open. More not than open. They didn't make the payments. So we figured the only thing to do was take it back and run it," she said with some resignation but no bitterness.

Kenneth was sinewy, thin faced, unshaven, wearing blue jeans and plaid shirt, with rough, disheveled hair, and an initial reserve that disappeared completely when conversation began. Ellen was white haired and grandmotherly, as I remembered my own grandmother, calm, slow, and gracious. (Before I left, two of her grandchildren wandered in the back door and out the front.) I had to remind myself not to romanticize their life, but I couldn't help it. Both seemed so entirely themselves, to have settled into Nowhere as their own place on the loneliest road.

"A motel needs to go in for this place to be profitable, but we are not up to it," Kenneth said, with a gesture of the arm that seemed to indicate a lack of energy as well as a lack of funds. "That's for some younger ones to do."

It was hard for me to imagine how Nowhere Cafe could be more attractive, by itself in a vast dry land, with a name that spoke where it was. To be isolated in the midst of desolation, to be lonely in a great land of loneliness! "Yes, Jeannette," I thought, remembering her question to me way back there at Nevada Beach and being utterly unable not to romanticize my own life. "I travel to get Nowhere." Apparently, on that day, no one else did. A number of cars drove by. None stopped. All had someplace to go.

April 22, 1994   Home Farm, south of 50
Writing this at the table in the duplex. Val Taylor lives in the other half. This half
is used for guests. It's nice. The best room I've found anywhere in the vicinity of
50: solid bed, firm pillows, hard shower, cool cross breeze. I spent most of the af-
ternoon interviewing Val and John B. Free, meeting some other people, and then
eating a great spaghetti dinner with leftover chocolate birthday cake for dessert.

VAL: Home Farm is the headquarters of the School of the Natural Order.
The School was founded many years ago by Vitvan, which means
"One Who Knows" in Sanskrit. His English name was Ralph Moriarty deBit, a Methodist-raised Kansas farm boy who was drawn to the
West. Somewhere in Oregon in the twenties he went to a lecture by
an East Indian named Mozumdar, who came down the aisle and said
to him, "I've been waiting for you. I've been sent to find an American
to work with." DeBit went through a seven-year cycle of study with
Mozumdar, who gave him the name of Vitvan.

    The primary purpose of the school is the publication and distribu-
tion of Vitvan's books and lesson courses. We have over two hundred
hours of lectures, most of which have been transcribed into lesson-
course form. We do no advertising and no proselytizing.

    My simplified explanation of the Natural Order is that an elm tree
is going to produce an elm tree, and so forth with other plants and animals until you get to the human species. Often before a baby is born,
the Daddy and Mommy have plans for this child that are imposed
from the outside.

DR: What today is called parental scripting?

VAL: Yes. Vitvan said you have to take your own journey. What we have
here is a school. Vitvan provided a curriculum. He says to each person, "It is hard work, and you've got to do it on your own."

DR: This was not his first community, is that right?

VAL: He started out in Bailey, Colorado. He wasn't a good businessman, so he lost that land. He went into Denver, and then during World War II lived on his wife's farm in North Carolina. After the war he bought land in San Diego County.

DR: Why did he leave San Diego?

VAL: One of his students was touring and came by here. She said to Vitvan, "I've found the ideal place for you." "Oh, I'm too old to move," he said. Then a navy plane hit the side of a hill near them. He was concerned about a third world war.

JOHN: We need to go back and put Vitvan in historical context: If there were a nuclear holocaust, he wanted to be as far away from city centers as possible.

VAL: This land was for sale by Mr. Fielding, Ellen's dad, the Ellen up at Nowhere Cafe. Vitvan lived here from 1957 to 1964, when he died. He is buried in the cemetery here. He never called himself "Master." Within himself, he was very clear, that it was not him, but the teachings.

DR: How are things going without him?

VAL: Well, we're here! One of our members said, "It is a miracle we have survived when you consider that we are a group of anarchists."

DR: There must be agreement on some large practical issues.

VAL: Not really. John has a real investment in how the land is cared for. I do not. Sometimes things get resolved and sometimes they don't. People say, "I want to go and be a part of that community." Then they get here, and we are not high-flown spiritual beings. We are ordinary, nitty-gritty, run-of-the-mill American citizens.

DR: What about disagreements over doctrine?

VAL: Well, in some sense, we don't have any doctrine. We are each an energy field, and this is an energy universe. That's loose enough.

DR: In the material that you gave me to read, I noticed a lot of gnostic elements.

JOHN: Vitvan wanted to carry on the tradition of the body of gnosis.

VAL: The gnostic tradition is the body of knowledge that helps us understand the evolution of humanity, that leads us to talk openly about transcending the physical. We are more than our bodies. The body is the tool with which we work through this incarnation. We build a new personality, a new psyche, every time around.

DR: So something survives the death of the body?

VAL: Vitvan called the process "palengenesis," like the leaves coming off the trees and blooming out again. The life germ, the energy system that I am, comes back in another . . . well, even if you say "form," that sounds like reincarnation. We don't believe that we are going to come back as dogs, but Val as Val is not going to come back. Personality does not survive. The qualities that I build in or refine do. This helps me make sense of why I am here and working so hard to get better.

DR: So there is some notion of evolution, of moving to higher and higher states?

VAL: Absolutely.

DR: Is there a final state?

VAL: In some Eastern traditions they believe in getting off the wheel. Well, that may be, but I don't know anyone who is ready to get off. Vitvan didn't believe that he was ready. We are all far, far from that point.

April 23, 1994   Home Farm, south of 50
Back in the duplex, musing, after a deluxe breakfast of homemade waffles. I like these people. I like the way they accept how ordinary they are. What they have accomplished at Home Farm is impressive. But to join them? To go out in the desert and join an intentional community there, one that seems to be going Somewhere, one that sees a goal at the end of all our travelling? Can't believe it. Can't do it. Today it's back on 50.

I learned about Mt. Moriah from Val and John at Home Farm. I told them I had been in Great Basin National Park and had climbed Mt. Wheeler.

"Oh," they responded, "Wheeler is not the power peak around here. Moriah is. That's it over there on the other side of 50. Have you been up it?"

"No," I said. But soon afterwards I decided to give it a try. To the south of the Loneliest Road was a religious community. I had visited it and decided it offered me no alternate route. What about this great mountain to the north, where I could gather a community of my mountaineering friends? What might I see from its summit? Home Farm and Mt. Moriah were directly across from one another. The roads to both turned off of 50 at Nowhere Cafe, in opposite directions.

Jeannette and I arrived at Nowhere Cafe at 4:15. Kenneth and Ellen were there, with one son and two grandsons. Within minutes Andrew Kirk from Davis and Michael and Valerie Cohen from Cedar City, Utah, pulled in at precisely the same time. Kirk was a lecturer at the University of California, Davis, an expert on Shakespeare. Michael Cohen, who teaches at Southern Utah State University in Cedar City, is the author of *The Pathless Way*, the best book I have ever read on John Muir. Valerie Cohen is an established painter of Great Basin landscapes. Sean O'Grady from Boise, D Jones from Berkeley, and Harold Glasser from Davis were ahead of us. Glasser was a graduate student at Davis in applied science and an expert in the philosophy of deep ecologist Arne Næss. He invited Jones to join us. An hour behind us were David Rothenberg, professor at the New Jersey Institute of Technology and editor of *Terra Nova,* and three more Davis graduate students, Mark Hoyer, Maryann Owens, and Stephanie Sarver, all four of whom were in Hoyer's Roadrunner. By 6:30 all had assembled at the trailhead beside Hampton Creek, twenty-one gravel miles to the north.

May 26, 1995   Mt. Moriah, north of 50

Everyone else in bed beside Hampton Creek a little over 7,000 feet on the side of Moriah. Moonless night. Stars overhead. Fire going out. From the NE a mildly ominous cloud reaches out in our direction. After all of us had arrived tonight, after tents were up and dinner eaten, I realized how important the group was. That it was not just me out here. Wilderness could be a place for communal activity, all of us exchanging with each other and with land and weather and rain and snow and stars. Fusion.

I signed the register kept by the National Forest Service. *Name*: Robertson party. *Number*: Twelve. *Destination*: Summit of Moriah. It was easy going for the first mile on an old mining road. The level of difficulty leapt one quantum the next mile. The road ended and the trail began to cross and recross a most swollen Hampton Creek. Sometimes the creek was the trail. We had to build rock bridges and push though underbrush that grabbed protruding snowshoes and skis. At 8,200 feet we began to see patches of snow. In another half mile and another 400 feet the amount of difficulty increased by another quantum. When the snow became too deep and too soft to walk on, we strapped on snowshoes. But then we couldn't get across the creek a hundred yards up the trail. So we unstrapped snowshoes. But then we couldn't get through the snow.

May 27, 1995   Mt. Moriah

Up late, feeding little sticks into a small fire, about 8,800 ft. on the eastern flank of Moriah. Everyone else already in tents. Snow is everywhere, except in small circular patches under large conifers. That's where the tents are, nine of them, spread out over an acre or so of an almost level ledge, each in a bare spot, each bare spot occupied. No vacancy at the Mt. Moriah Motel.

The next morning, while the snow was still crunchy, the Energetic Five headed up Hampton Creek in search of the summit. By the time I unzipped my way out of a three-season tent, the Cohens had eaten and packed. They were go-ing back. They might, they said, head for home once they reached the trailhead. Overnight altitude sickness had sketched its lines into Sarver's face. She and Owens left an hour later, Hoyer, Jeannette, and I an hour after that. The group had spread out all along the trail.

Lots of clouds, a little rain, a little snow, a little sun. Just as I was packing camera away from an hour's photo session about a mile above the trailhead, Rothenberg appeared, then Jones and Glasser, then O'Grady and Kirk. They had reached the Table, a couple of miles and 1,000 feet from the summit. They got a glimpse of it. Clouds then covered it. They turned back.

May 28, 1995   Nowhere Cafe
Fission. I knew before I reached the cars that Michael and Valerie would be gone. They were. The rest of us stood around debating to stay or not to stay. I didn't want to leave, but did not say so. Instead asked everyone else what they wanted to do. All wanted to go. "Not another wet night." "But it looks like clearing," I said, almost hopefully, hoping almost to persuade. "Yeah, sure!" So we left, with such resolve that we forgot to say good-bye to D and Harold, who were parked around a bend and out of sight.

I had imagined nothing human at the border. Maybe a sign of welcome to Utah in one direction and welcome to Nevada in the other, but that's all. Nothing else but borderless sand and sage. From miles away I could tell I was right about the vegetation and wrong about humans. A speck of trees, a building, no, two buildings. I counted down the miles, 6, 5, 4, 3, 2, 1, 0. I got out of the car on the north side of the road and sighted south down the boundary line, exactly defined by the crease in the pavement where the Nevada crew stopped laying asphalt and the Utah crew began. In Utah was the Border Inn Motel. In Nevada, snuggled right up to the line, was the Border Inn Cafe. The reason for this arrangement was not hard to guess. One border, one business, two states with different tolerances for gaming.

The rules of the game I was playing said turn around here. Take Highway 50. Make an incision where Nevada meets California and another at the Utah line. Lift this section out and go back and forth. Do not get off of Highway 50, at least not far off. Do not go past Nevada. This game does not make much sense. Precisely on that very point, it may, however, most imitate life. At this time in the late twentieth century and in this landscape of hybrid cultures, life itself seems all too much like a game, one in which the rules are arbitrary, made up by each of us, alone. And the Nevada-Utah border may be an apt metaphor for death, which rarely comes for each of us in our loneliness at the moment we have reached a meaningful destination, such as the summit of a range. It is just out there on the level, where someone else put it for reasons that are extraneous to our journey.

Much of the poignancy of life arises from the fact that the game we all play has two sets of lines. One set we draw by making up our lives. The other set is given, by genes and culture, by time and place, by the inherent structures of the universe. We want with quiet desperation to see the two sets as one, the way our eyes by focusing make one image out of two. But rarely, it seems, do we manage it.

May 28, 1995   On the Road
Heading west toward Ely, rising out of one basin to cross another range. All the others are gone, to Boise, to Cedar City, to New York City. Those going to Davis are miles in front of us. As we gained elevation I glanced back over my right shoulder in the direction of Moriah. There it was, a shinny white ridge rising to a rounded top. A promise. From here no more than a promise that I had not come close to realizing. I pulled the Honda over and got out. Jeannette got out. I put the fully automatic Olympus on zoom and took a couple of pictures. We got back in the car and pulled out once again onto 50.

Border Inn and Cafe. 1994. Silver Print.

Nowhere Cafe. 1994. Silver Print.

Open Range. 1994. Silver Print.

Abandoned. 1994. Silver Print.

GARY SNYDER & JACK KEROUAC ON MOUNT TAMALPAIS

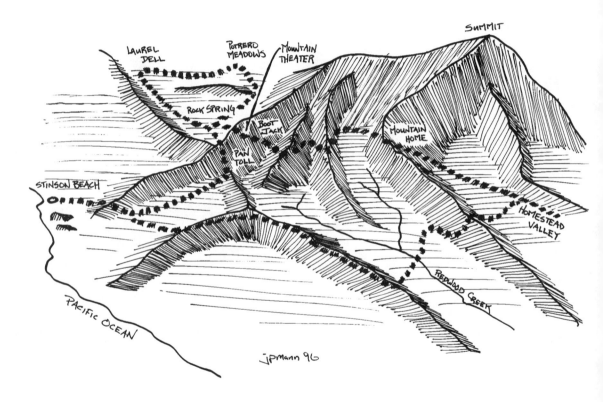

SUMMIT

LAUREL DELL

POTRERO MEADOWS

MOUNTAIN THEATER

ROCK SPRING

BOOT JACK

PAN TOLL

MOUNTAIN HOME

HOMESTEAD VALLEY

STINSON BEACH

REDWOOD CREEK

PACIFIC OCEAN

jprmann 96

CHAPTER FOUR

The Closer You Get to Real Matter

REAL MATTER

On May 1, 1956, Gary Snyder and Jack Kerouac sat on the upper stone seats of the Greek-style Mountain Theater on the southern slopes of Mt. Tamalpais. They had paused to rest on their two-day, round-trip hike from Mill Valley to Stinson Beach. While Kerouac rubbed his feet and munched on an orange, Snyder exclaimed, "The closer you get to real matter, rock air fire wood, boy, the more spiritual the world is" (Kerouac 1958, 206). This sentence states what is perhaps not only the central idea of Gary Snyder's poetry and prose, but the fixed point around which rotate the thought and practice of many who take to trails. If one habit beats in the ritual heart of their lives and their literature, surely this is it: the practice of "mattering," of repeatedly accessing the thing that is at one and the same time both spirit and matter. "No Ideas but in Things," says W. C. Williams, an important literary and spiritual ancestor. "No Matter, Never Mind," says the title of one of Snyder's poems.

From his first visit to Mt. Tamalpais at the age of nine until the present, Snyder has continually practiced on the mountain, practiced bringing himself progressively closer to this dominant rock north of San Francisco Bay, thrust up by the collision of the Pacific and North American plates. Initially he practiced, in another sense of the word, by taking short exploratory hikes. Then in 1956 and again in 1965, he tied together pieces of different trails into two round-trip ritual journeys on the mountain. The first was an informal overnight hike with Jack Kerouac. The second was a formal circumambulation with Allen Ginsberg and Philip Whalen.

Snyder's first trip to Tamalpais was in the summer of 1939, when he took the train by himself from the state of Washington to Richmond, California, where his aunt lived. He remembers vividly her taking him not only to the San Francisco World's Fair, but to Muir Woods, Muir Beach, and Mt. Tamalpais. He came again in the fall of 1948. Earlier that year he had hitchhiked to New York City in order to earn some money on the high seas. After a round-trip to South America, he thumbed his way back across the continent to San Francisco, where he met his girlfriend from Reed College, Robin Collins, who was living in the city with her mother on Lyons Street. Over the Labor Day weekend he and Collins took the Greyhound bus to Pan Toll, and from there packed over the shoulder where Rock Springs is and down to Lagunitas Reservoir. They camped there for a couple of nights before hiking down a dirt road to Bolinas, where they caught a bus back to the city.

He saw the mountain next in 1952, when he moved to the Bay Area from Bloomington, Indiana, where he had been a graduate student in anthropology at the University of Indiana. His father was building a house in Corte Madera, at the foot of Tamalpais, and Snyder did carpentry work for him on the weekends. In his spare time he began to explore Tamalpais's extensive system of trails, a process that went on sporadically for the next three years.

Then, in January of 1956, he moved into a cabin up the slope from the house that Locke McCorkle rented at 370 Montford Avenue in Homestead Valley, a rather steep, subdivided ravine about a mile long, situated at the foot of Tamalpais in a south-southeasterly direction from East Peak. Since the landlord did not know of Snyder's occupation of the property, he was able to stay there rent-free. This cabin was fairly large, with three rooms. It was apparently built by an elderly man, who, however, did not live to finish the job. It had, for example, no interior paneling and no doors. McCorkle's brother-in-law had made some minor improvements, like placing burlap over the exposed studs and installing a wood stove, but he moved away before moving in. Snyder immediately set about fixing it up. He made weather-tight living quarters for himself by putting sheets of plastic-coated chicken wire in the windows and doors of one of the rooms. On the burlap walls he hung prints of Chinese silk paintings, maps of the Marin area and of Washington State, and various poems he had written. Around the room he stationed old clay pots full of freshly picked flowers from the yard, and covered the floor with straw mats. On his own personal mat he laid a mattress covered with a paisley shawl. Each day he rolled up his sleeping bag and placed it at the head of the mattress. The room reflected its inhabitant's sense of simplicity and discipline.

During the winter and early spring of that year, Snyder frequently scrambled up the steep bushy slope at the western end of Homestead Valley to the intersection of Edgewood Avenue and Sequoia Valley Road. From there the entire mountain was accessible to him. He took Dipsea Trail, which passed through this intersection on its way down into Muir Woods and over the hills to Stinson Beach. By any number of spurs he ascended Tam's southern and western flanks to places like Pan Toll Station and Rock Springs. And he went directly up East Peak via Mountain Home. By April he had thoroughly explored the mountain in small bites and had mapped out a series of trails by which he could take it in as a whole.

In early April Jack Kerouac arrived at McCorkle's. He and Snyder had met the preceding year in San Francisco and had climbed Matterhorn Peak the previous October. Not long after that Kerouac had returned to the East Coast to stay with his sister and mother in North Carolina. While there he received a letter from Snyder inviting him to share the Homestead Valley cabin. He had also applied for and received an appointment as a fire lookout in the North Cascades. So in March he set out across the country once again to be with Snyder and to be closer to his summer job in Washington.

The two spent a nearly idyllic month together in the cabin, the spell broken only by a few arguments, mainly over Kerouac's drinking, but also over Snyder's suspicion that Kerouac talked Buddhism without experiencing it. It is also clear that Snyder's preoccupation over his upcoming trip to Japan often irritated Kerouac. Snyder instructed Kerouac in the art of wood cutting, they prepared dinners for each other, discussed Buddhism together, and received guests, a list of whom reads like a Who's Who of the San Francisco Literary Renaissance: Allen Ginsberg, Philip Whalen, Kenneth Rexroth, Michael McClure, Robert Creeley, and Philip Lamantia, among others. And also they partied, every weekend.

All of these parties were practice for the big one, which came in late April, a three-day farewell extravaganza for Snyder. It was, as were most of the Homestead parties that month, a tripartite affair. Down the hill inside McCorkle's house the guests, including Snyder's father, danced to records and to the beat of Kerouac playing bongo drums on inverted cans. Out in the yard, to the tune of live guitar music and in the light of a bonfire, Rexroth held forth on the state of American poetry, concluding that, outside of present company, William Carlos Williams was the only poet around worth reading. Meanwhile, couples continually drifted off up the hill and into the cabin.

As the wine went down, the clothes came off. At one point Allen Ginsberg and Peter Orlovsky (both naked) stood talking with Rexroth and Alan Watts (both clothed), the four having a normal conversation about world affairs. As nude bodies whirled on the dance floor, Kerouac sat off to one side cross-legged, either pounding out bongo rhythms or talking Buddhism with Claude Dalenburg. Although he sometimes "looked at all that flesh and licked [his] lips in secret" (177), and even teased Snyder about the surplus of women present, he maintained his position as observer, as was his custom.

Snyder's comportment during the party was the opposite of Kerouac's in every way imaginable. If Kerouac's mode was detachment, his was engagement. Several times during the previous month he had come home to find Kerouac doing nothing. To his query of "Why did you sit around all day?" Kerouac would answer, "I am the Buddha known as the Quitter" (180) or, punning on the Daoist concept of nonactivity, "I practice do-nothing" (175). To this last remark Snyder's answer was apt and accurate, "My Buddhism is activity." So at the party he ate and drank, danced and stripped, and in general had a good time.

THE HIKE

By the third day, however, Snyder was tired of partying, and he and Kerouac sneaked off early in the morning for two days of hiking on Mt. Tamalpais, as they had arranged to do before the festivities began. They followed Montford Road and Laverne Street to the western end of Homestead Valley and ascended to Edgewood Road, more or less following the route of what is today called Cowboy Rock Trail. Switchbacks took them through oxalis blooming, across several bridges over the creek bed, and through a sunny upper meadow to Edgewood Road. They followed it and Pipeline Trail to Mountain Home, where they crossed Panorama Highway and joined Troop 80 Trail.

For two miles they contoured along the southern slope of Tamalpais past Van Wyck Meadow and then went up past Bootjack Picnic Grounds to "Mountain Theater hot white Greek rock bowl" via Easy Grade, "scaring a winded Doe breathing already great pants" along the way (Snyder 1956; unless otherwise indicated, all descriptions of the hike are taken from this source). Here they paused long enough for Kerouac to cool his feet and eat an orange before crossing the highway to Rock Springs. Benstein Trail took them through "real Manzanita brush and Live Oak" to Potrero Meadow, where they unpacked, made tea, and slept in the sun.

Leaving Kerouac behind, Snyder went alone to Barth's Retreat "and being curious went on along Mickey O'Brien Trail to Laurel Dell a lovely flat meadow glowing green in the afternoon sun and a good camp." He chastised himself for being so depressed by the course of human history: "Nature is inexhaustible, why should I fret at a few years of men?" He followed the fire road back to Potrero Meadow, finding a puffball along the way. Slowly and with meditation, he and Jack built a fire and cooked dinner. It consisted of "Green pea soup with scraps of fried bacon & bacon grease throwed [sic] in, Boiled bulghour with mixed dried vegetables and bacon throwed in, fried small sausage pats, tea, sliced fried puffball, dried fruit for dessert." After dinner, he rolled a cigarette and smoked it as the two of them talked quietly by the fire late into the night.

After a breakfast of oatmeal with apricot mush and tea, and after Snyder bandaged a toe blistered the day before because he chose to hike without socks on, they retraced his route to Laurel Dell. Turning south, they followed Cataract Trail "in a gulch of Fir and Maple and mossy rocks" back to Rock Springs, crossed the highway and descended to Pan Toll. It was a clear day with fog only to the west, so they paused often to scan the cities around the bay. Down Steep Ravine they switchbacked through the redwoods to the junction of Dipsea Trail, where they hid their packs before continuing on to Stinson Beach.

Jack talked the clerk at the grocery store into selling him a bottle of "poorboy port" for thirty-seven cents instead of the marked price of forty cents. Port in hand they went past Seadowns and past some rocks to a cove where Snyder had been before. The tide was out and curlews fed on the flats. They drank the wine and "got Chinese-poet-drunk" while munching on Rye-Krisp and salami. After a swim and a nap, they recrossed Highway 1, retrieved their packs from hiding, and took a rollercoasting Dipsea Trail to Muir Woods. By this time Kerouac was dead tired and longed for Homestead Valley. All he could think of was munching a Hershey Bar. This apparent retreat from the spiritual into the material obviously irritated Snyder, who exclaimed, "There's your Buddhism, a Hershey bar. How about moonlight in an orange grove and a vanilla ice-cream cone?" (Kerouac, 212). From the "deep glade tourist trails" of Muir Woods they climbed cross-country to Sun Trail, all the while dodging the ubiquitous poison oak. While Kerouac rested, Snyder listened to "some sparrow bird give notes, identically repeated far away." Sun Trail took them through "the richest flower field, steep hillside meadow, of all" to Windy Gap. From there, "in the afternoon long shadow, down Bayview Road and other roads" they "limped on home." No sooner there than Snyder went out to buy groceries, over Kerouac's protests of, "Oh, man, aren't you tired? Just go to bed, we'll eat tomorrow." He returned bearing a gift of three Hershey Bars (Kerouac, 213).

June 13, 1992   El Rebozo's, Mill Valley

I lean back against the hard, uncomfortable board that passes for a chair, trying to put sore back at rest, waiting for order of flautas, here at the intersection of Highway 1 and Freeway 101. Spent the day taking pictures in the area of Rock Springs and the Mountain Theater. Now mulling over what getting closer to real matter means to me personally. After a year of snapping shutter on the slopes of Tam, what do the photographs say back to me? I hear:

> *Petroglyph, archetype, shaman*
> *and the gesture of dance—archaic*
> *animal, animalistic, animistic*

Words that take me back in culture to the neolithic and back in evolution to the mammal, sounds that carry energy and exuberance, syllables that bind the human together with the animal, vegetable, and mineral.

Snyder did not take to the trails of Tamalpais in order to escape, hermit style, from the farewell party and the drinking and sex that went on there, even though Kerouac has him say as the hike begins, "Goddammit it feels good to get away from dissipation and go in the woods" (200). As an expression of relief at being free from the frantic pace of the party, this statement may be accurate, but it definitely does not reflect Snyder's fundamental attitude. To drink and to dance with your friends—these are no less valid ways of accessing the spiritual through the physical than trekking through the woods. We would need to add "flesh" to "rock air fire wood" before this list would truly represent his thinking.

Nevertheless, being on the trail does represent a kind of freedom for Snyder. This freedom is not from the material world, much less from the world of social and sexual intercourse. It is, rather, escape from an attitude toward material things, from a bondage to American capitalism and the consumption of products that it encourages. At Snyder's cottage in Berkeley the previous fall, when Philip Whalen and Allen Ginsberg joined Kerouac and Snyder in an evening of crazy, visionary conversation, the entire group imagined an apocalyptic ending to the present political and economic world order. According to Kerouac the dialogue went as follows. Coughlin is Whalen, Alvah is Ginsberg, Japhy is Snyder, and the speaker is Kerouac himself. Snyder began,

> "Handcuffs will get soft and billy clubs will topple over, let's go on being free anyhow."
> "The President of the United States suddenly grows crosseyed and floats away!" I yell.
> "And anchovies will turn to dust!" yells Coughlin.
> "The Golden Gate is creaking with sunset rust," says Alvah.
> "And anchovies will turn to dust," insists Coughlin.
> "Give me another slug of that jug. How! Ho! Hoo!" Japhy leaping

up: "I've been reading Whitman, know what he says, *Cheer up slaves, and horrify foreign despots,* he means that's the attitude for the Bard, the Zen Lunacy bard of old desert paths, see the whole thing is a world full of rucksack wanderers, Dharma Bums refusing to subscribe to the general demand that they consume production and therefore have to work for the privilege of consuming, all that crap they didn't really want anyway such as refrigerators, TV sets, cars, at least new fancy cars, certain hair oils and deodorants and general junk you finally always see a week later in the garbage anyway, all of them imprisoned in a system of work, produce, consume, work, produce, consume, I see a vision of a great rucksack revolution thousands or even millions of young Americans wandering around with rucksacks, going up to mountains to pray, making children laugh and old men glad, making young girls happy and old girls happier, all of 'em Zen Lunatics who go about writing poems that happen to appear in their heads for no reason and also by being kind and also by strange unexpected acts keep giving visions of eternal freedom to everybody and to all living creatures." (97–98)

Hiking for Snyder is a way of furthering a political, social, and spiritual revolution. The ground of all right living (one of the meanings of *dharma*) is, literally, the ground we walk on. Hiking at one and the same time frees us from a dependency on nonessential things (the products of humans) and grounds us in "rock air fire wood" (the products of *dharma* in another of its senses). The essential nature of things is not an Aristotelian plot nor a Hegelian dialectic, and does not lead to a goal. Therefore, it cannot be the object of a quest, as for the grail. Instead, it goes round and round and on and on, rather like the hike that Kerouac and Snyder took and even more like the poem that Snyder projected writing and told Kerouac about as they walked:

Know what I'm gonna do? I'll do a new long poem called "Rivers and Mountains Without End" and just write it on and on on a scroll and unfold on and on with new surprises and always what went before forgotten, see, like a river, or like one of them real long Chinese silk paintings that show two little men hiking in an endless landscape of gnarled old trees and mountains so high they merge with the fog in the upper silk void. (200)

That Kerouac in *Dharma Bums* is accurately reporting Snyder's thought is confirmed by Snyder himself and is further demonstrated by entries in his journals of 1955 and 1956. For example, on April 24, 1955, he wrote that "there is endless fascination & delight to be found in the simple perception & contemplation of matter." In the same vein, a portion of the entry for June 11 reads, "A Tree. A Rock. A Cloud. Start with the simplest." Then, later in the year, on November 13, in one of numerous attempts to define Nirvana, he noted that "THIS WORLD viewed with love & detachment, is *nirvana.*" It became clear to Snyder that the mundane could simultaneously be spiritual only if it existed inside as well as outside the individual human being. On August 27, in Yosemite for the summer working on trails north of the Tuolumne River, he wrote, "I am not able to see it or know it—this enormous inhuman beauty—and yet, letting go, I am simply it, being part of it, in me as well as outside." And on May 7, 1956, aboard the *Arita Maru,* a week after the excursion with Kerouac, he reflected on his distinctive perspective as a person and as an artist: "It seems the inhuman world of nature is my clearest vision."

The hike Snyder took with Kerouac on May 1–2, 1956, was, in several interesting ways, prophetic. It was like throwing a piece of real matter into the lake of his future: the splash caused waves that spread out through the rest of his life. By withdrawing from his friends gathered for a farewell party, he anticipated his leaving the United States for Japan. He also "practiced" forsaking the quotidian for a more austere routine: two days of backpacking would soon become the far more demanding regimen of a lay monk in a Zen temple in Kyoto. The hike was, in addition, both in its circular form and its content of "real matter" on a spiritual mountain, an imitation of the life he wanted to lead as a "Zen lunatic." The hike even enacted the type of poetry Snyder wanted to write, poems that "show little men hiking" in a landscape "Without End." In all of these ways his trek over the slopes of Tamalpais was a kind of initiation, a rite of passage.

In contrast to Snyder's atheistic spiritual materialism and his vision of *bhikkus* redeeming the world by an accumulation of little acts of kindness, Kerouac remained true to his Christian upbringing. However much he may have used Buddhist terminology, beneath the skin, and maybe not too far beneath, he was French Catholic. So, on the Mt. Tamalpais hike, Kerouac responded to the presence of suffering in the world in distinctively Christian terms: "Japhy, do you think God made the world to amuse himself because he was bored? Because if so he would have to be mean." When Snyder asked who this God might be, Kerouac immediately switched to Buddhist nomenclature: "Just Tathagata, if you will." Snyder then gave him a lesson in Buddhist doctrine: "Well it says in the sutra that God, or Tathagata, doesn't himself emanate a world from his womb but it just appears due to the ignorance of sentient beings." Kerouac, however, was not satisfied and, although he had apparently abandoned Christian vocabulary, restated his concern in concepts that make sense only if Ultimate Reality has intentionality: "But he emanated the sentient beings and their ignorance too. It's all too pitiful. I ain't gonna rest till I find out *why*, Japhy, *why*" (201).

Kerouac's notion of redemption is also thoroughly Christian: in order to turn humankind's suffering into joy, the chosen ones must suffer vicariously. In *Dharma Bums* and *On the Road* the chosen ones are those "beaten" by the American capitalist system, the down-and-out, the outcasts, the bums, including, of course, Kerouac himself, who wanted most of all to be a saint suffering for the world. This mind-set reveals itself continually in *Dharma Bums*, even when the context is not religious. So, at the beginning of their trek, he likened the two hikers to pack animals. In the context of the entire book, as well as in the context of Kerouac's thought as a whole, the backpacks they carry symbolize a spiritual "burden." It is not, however, their own sins on their backs. They are not pilgrims progressing towards the Heavenly City, but Christs loaded with the crosses of others. Although Kerouac uses the plural in the following paragraph, it is abundantly clear that he speaks for himself, not Snyder. "As ever I strode on behind him and when we began to climb, with our packs feeling good on our backs as though we were pack animals and didn't feel right without a burden, it was that same old lonesome old good old thwap thwap up the trail, slowly, a mile an hour" (200).

In the Judeo-Christian tradition, wild nature is not itself the secret at the heart of the universe. It is the locus only, not the substance of revelation. In terms of the content of what Moses learned on Mt. Sinai, or what John the Baptist and Jesus learned in the desert, place was incidental. In the Bible, wilderness is a convenient place for epiphany because one is less distracted there. The same is true for Kerouac. Mt. Tamalpais did not teach him anything of note. He liked being reminded by the heavy pack that he was a human beast of spiritual burdens. He enjoyed the conversation and the views. He was impressed with Snyder's prowess but was totally dependent upon him for food, shelter, and direction. Jack's beat was the city, where "the public" (201) danced a painful existence in step with mechanical, not natural, rhythms. It is hardly surprising, then, that when he returned to Laurel Dell after Snyder's departure for Japan, he got lost several times and became so lonely that he stayed only one night (Nicosia, 526).

July 14, 1992   Mickey O'Brien Trail

Strangely, it's the Hershey Bars I keep coming back to.

Sean O'Grady and I left Homestead Valley early this morning to rehike the Snyder-Kerouac route of May 1–2, 1956. Went by Mountain Home and Mountain Theater and through Potrero Meadow. Slowed down and stopped to take in the beauty of the Mickey O'Brien trail between Barth's Retreat and Laurel Dell. Here is one of the wildest paths on Mt. Tamalpais: lush growth sponsored by the fog that blows in from the Pacific. Last December when I was here it floated calmly through the tops of the red-barked madrone and the droop-branched Douglas fir. This day it is out to sea.

I look down at the creek bed some fifty feet below, at the moss-covered fallen limbs and termite-eaten rotting trunks, and up through a tangled maze of twisted limbs. If the ancient order of nature is to be found in Marin County, it is here. Rock, air, and wood are close, and fire in this multiyear period of drought seems not far away. Yet, like a recurring melody, I cannot get the three Hershey Bars out of my head. Could it be that the closer you get to a Hershey Bar, the more spiritual the world is?

The only thoughtful answer to this question is surely yes. It is my impression that, with virtual unanimity, the religions of the world affirm the potential holiness of all mundane objects. Bringing the Hershey Bars from the local grocery store to Jack Kerouac was one of those "strange unexpected acts" of kindness Snyder believes Dharma Bums should distribute everywhere to all people. In that moment, potential spiritual energy became actualized. In Snyder's terms, those chocolate bars became "real matter."

While all who follow trails into the mountains may admit that "spirit" lies within the Hershey Company's most famous product waiting to be released by an act of kindness, few would assert that a candy bar is as likely to become "real" as the phenomena of nature are. So we have a conundrum: all objects are holy but some are more holy than others. I doubt this double knot can be untied either by logical manipulation or by appeal to authority. Indeed, I wonder if it is not always after the fact that we tie the knot in the first place. In actual and immediate experience, we all know where and when and by what we are most likely to be moved. Snyder himself had no doubt about his own predilections, even if their origin was somewhat mysterious to him. An extended journal entry from January 18, 1954, reads as follows:

114

> Walking out of the Olympics in 1950: the sudden realization of order & chaos, chaos in nature: the paths and gardens are not trimmed and ordered. Everything falls everwhich way, the birds swoop all directions, the deer go crashing off through the brush, & the glaciers fall down & smash the trees: but NOTHING IS OUT OF PLACE.
>
> That is why they say: The Tao is like (=)? Nature.
>
> Here is a koan for you. order & chaos. . . .
>
> 1952: Jim Baxter, Harold Vail and I in Frank Beebe's old cabin, up Ruby, at the fork of Canyon and Granite Creek, July, a hot-night thunderstorm, stood in the warm rain in the cabin door, counting the strikes on the ridges. The most pleasant days I can recall have been walking in mountains, mostly alone.
>
> why?? did I at so early an age become a nature-mystic? it wa'nt anything I read?? what did it. This puzzles me. . . .
>
> I wdn't trade all the poetry & philosophy this world ever produced for 1 summer day on the Dosewallips.

Thus, it is hardly surprising when Snyder includes only natural objects when he makes his oracular announcement to Kerouac on the steps of the Mountain Theater: earth, air, fire, wood. We would all agree with him, Yes, "the inhuman world of nature is [your] clearest vision."

My own predilections are largely consonant with Snyder's. Yet, because I am a literary historian as well as a photographer and lover of trails, my situation is somewhat more complicated. Sitting on the steps of the Mountain

Theater, I have to acknowledge that I am there because Snyder and Kerouac have been there before me. *Jack Kerouac Sat Here.* I have come to a natural place already marked out and interpreted by two human beings special to me. To Snyder's fourfold list, therefore, I have to add "the past," where the past refers to individual and communal remembrance and rehearsal of previous human activity in a place.

The closer you get to real matter—earth, air, fire, wood, yes, those primarily, but also Hershey Bars and past events—the more spiritual the world is.

The Closer
You Get to
Real Matter

Exercise in Orientation #11. 1991. Polaroid Print.

Rock Face #1. 1992. Polaroid Print.

Power Stick #22. 1993. Polaroid Print.

Bush Man #14. 1995. Polaroid Print.

THE CIRCUMAMBULATION OF MOUNT TAMALPAIS

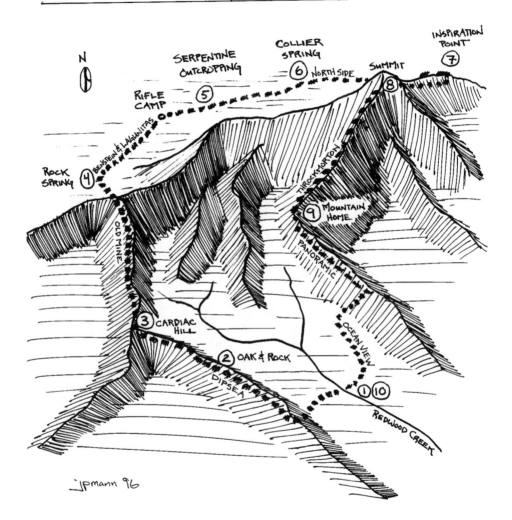

jpmann 96

CHAPTER FIVE

Coming Round the Mountain

BEFORE

Late 1980s   Davis

Had lunch today at the Coffee House with student from Wilderness Lit class. We sat at a table near the entrance to the bakery. He said, "I know what to do in the city, not just to fill up time, but to experience the place. I go out on a trail, and I'm at a loss. It's different, all right. The scenery is grand. [Here he waved his hand in a sweeping arc above his head.] But what do I do? How do I make nature happen to me?"

STAGE 1

First of all, Wild Things. Poison oak, ticks, and rattlesnakes inhabit Tamalpais. You don't want to touch the first; you don't want the other two to bite you. It is good luck when a rattlesnake visits you at a comfortable distance.

May 11, 1991   Redwood Creek, Muir Woods
Parked in the annex at Muir Woods. Two garbage cans were among us as we said, almost together, Lew Welch's "This is the last place to go." On the pavement, under the great, old California Bay, a few feet from where Dipsea Trail, on its way from town to town, crosses Redwood Creek, on its way from mountain to ocean.

This was where they gathered—Gary Snyder, Philip Whalen, and Allen Ginsberg—on October 22, 1965, to begin a formal circumambulation of Mt. Tamalpais. Before crossing the creek and heading west on the Dipsea Trail, they chanted the Heart of the Perfection of the Great Wisdom sutra (see appendix A) along with the *dharani* for removing disasters, and the Four Vows:

Beings are numberless: I vow to enlighten them.
Obstacles are countless: I vow to cut them down.
Dharma Gates are limitless: I vow to master them.
The Buddha-Way is endless: I vow to follow through.

                                        (*Translated by Gary Snyder*)

STAGE 2

Nature of Hike. Twelve miles round-trip, maybe fourteen. Elevation gain: 2,500 feet, done gradually. Elevation loss: 2,500 feet.

May 11, 1991   Rock and Oak
Across the creek and up and westwardly through a mixed-evergreen forest of
Doug firs and laurel and out onto rolling, low ridges covered with exotic annual
grasses. Random coyote bush. To a niche seat in a split rock under a coastal live
oak. Mark said, "David, you look natural there. Like you grew there."

"I don't know why we went that day instead of some other day," said
Philip Whalen, leaning back in his chair, head tilted slightly upward, scan-
ning his memory. We were sitting in his living room on the bottom floor of
the Hartford Street Zen Center, more properly known as *Issanji* (one
mountain temple). It was March 12, 1992. Gary Snyder and I had met at
REI on San Pablo Avenue in Berkeley at noon and had driven together over
the Bay Bridge and up Market Street to San Francisco's Castro District,
where the Zen Center is located. Whalen had been formally installed as ab-
bot on September 14, 1991. I had arranged the interview between the three
of us in order to get a historical perspective on the initial religious circumambulation of Mt. Tamalpais, roughly a fourteen-mile circuit of the mountain by Allen Ginsberg, Snyder, and Whalen on October 22, 1965. I had just
asked why they chose that date. At this point Snyder added, "It just happened to be the day we could all get together. But we did make a decision.
Let's all go do a formal circumambulation of Tamalpais and establish sacred
spots on it and pay our respects and do some chanting. Allen was doing a lot
of chanting at that time. So was I."

STAGE 3

Weather. A foggy morning followed by a sunny afternoon is most likely.
Dress in layers, maybe a long-sleeve shirt, a sweater, and a light jacket to
keep out wind and fog.

August 20, 1993   Cardiac Hill
Hot! Much hotter than I expected. I dressed for fog. I had to slow the pace. Re-

freshing to enter the woods. Some of my favorite plants along the trail: tan bark
oak, black huckleberry, monkey flower. Toe beginning to hurt. New Shoes.
Brought along old shoes in pack. Cindy carries her new baby on her back. Turkey
vulture overhead, going around. Joined by a jet. A bite of chocolate chip oatmeal
cookie that I baked from the Silver Palate Cookbook.

I was curious about beginnings. Where did the idea of a circumambulation of Mt. Tamalpais come from? In 1955 and 1956, before he departed for
the Orient, Snyder began to put pieces of trail together to make a circular
hiking route around Tamalpais. Likewise, Whalen circumnavigated the
mountain with Locke McCorkle in the late 1950s or early 1960s. Both
made it quite clear, however, that these outings were not, in Whalen's
words, "intentionally ceremonial." He continued, "We were just looking,
because it was fun, something nice to do." The first exposure either of them
had to *pradakshina,* the religious rite of circling clockwise a sacred object,
came during Snyder's first visit to Japan.

I got the idea of a circumambulatory, walking meditation, while I was
in Japan the first time and also from reading literature that mentioned
that kind of thing, literature about Far Eastern religious practices. I
think maybe the first time I heard about it was when I was in Kyoto
in 1956. I heard from Walter Nowick and others about the walking
practice on Mt. Hiei. Walter went on a walk with Horisawa Somon
one day and came back and reported what it was like. There was and
still is a practice on Mt. Hiei, called *gyodo,* "walking route" or "walking practice."

Snyder went on to explain his understanding of pradakshina and its origins:

There is the Buddhist practice of circumambulating a *stupa,* a burial
mound. This is a part of ancient Indo-European lore, Indo-Aryan lore,
that probably goes back to central Asia, and which includes the Celts.

Some of these people came down into India with these customs. There they made a burial mound of carved stone, and paid their respects to it by going around it, keeping it to the right, clockwise. In very early Buddhism, before they had any images of the Buddha, which at first was resisted, the centers of worship were burial mounds that supposedly had within them relics from the cremation of Buddha.

Either because of that, or as a parallel coming from some other line, was the practice of doing the same with and around mountains. They are both called pradakshina. In Buddhist lore there is both sitting meditation and walking meditation. Along the line, not universally, but here and there in India, China, and Japan, some of the Buddhist groups started circumambulatory/meditation routes on the mountains themselves. That was my understanding of it.

So, I used to hike around on Mt. Hiei a lot, and I walked the route that the monks walked. I never did it with them. I knew the route, and I knew all the shrines on it. I knew that they stopped at each of the shrines. And I knew that the same was true in other contexts [that is, on different mountains in other parts of the Far East], that there are stations as you go around. So, when I was back in this country, and there was a lot of woo-woo in the air anyway [laughs], it seemed like a good time to draft Mt. Tamalpais into our scheme [continues to chuckle].

STAGE 4

Essentials. Restrooms are available along the trail, though not necessarily strategically placed. Likewise with water, but you should bring a water bottle that will hold a quart. Also bring a lunch, hat, and sunglasses. Wear good hiking shoes.

May 11, 1991   Rock Springs
Hailed an old car with old man driver to take a sick Lenore back to Muir Woods. The air was so dense I thought I might be hit before being seen. Coni explained

our mission to him and introduced me by way of authentication. "David Robert-
son," he exclaimed, "I know you. The Yosemite author." "Harold Gilliam," I
said, "I know you. The Chronicle journalist."

On April 23, 1991, Snyder gave a guest lecture to a class I taught on the literature of wilderness. He emphasized how syncretic Ginsberg, Whalen, and
he were in the selection of chants for the initial circumambulation of Mt.
Tamalpais, "some traditional Buddhist ones, some Hindu mantras." He listed
four types. First of all was a statement of the "total truth of the universe" as
the three of them understood it. They chose the Heart of the Perfection of
the Great Wisdom Sutra. Second was a magic spell (dharani) that would push
disasters away and at the same time "spread protection and well-being
throughout the universe." They also selected short verses that addressed
specific powers: "rocks, animals, plants, human beings, watersheds, up-
thrusts, all spiritual beings." Finally, they recited the "Four Vows" of Buddhism, in order to "dedicate their lives to work for the benefit of every other
being on earth."

These chants were performed at various stations along the route around
Mt. Tamalpais. I was under the impression that the stations had been chosen
in advance on the basis of hikes Snyder had taken on Mt. Tamalpais in the
decade or so before 1965. Both he and Whalen assured me that I was mis-
taken. "We just felt the magic vibrations," he said, as Whalen chuckled. "We
decided on them the day that we walked it, by being finely tuned," a sentence punctuated by Whalen's "Right, right!"

Lunch at Rifle Camp
On May 11, 1991, I ate peanut butter and jelly sandwiches. Two of them.
Pringles. Oreos.

On August 20, 1993, I ate peanut butter and jelly sandwiches. Several.
Chocolate chip oatmeal cookies. A few green grapes from Stephanie. Water.
More water.

On October 22, 1965, Snyder, Whalen, and Ginsberg ate swiss cheese sandwiches, swede bread with liverwurst, salami, jack cheese, olives, gomoku-no-moto from a can, grapes, panetoni with apple currant jelly and sweet butter, oranges, and soujouki—Greek walnuts in grape-juice paste.

STAGE 5

Directions to trailhead. Take I-80 west from Davis. In about forty miles turn west on Highway 37 in Vallejo. Take 37 about twenty-five miles to Highway 101. Take 101 south about fifteen miles to Highway 1. Take Hwy. 1 about three and a half miles to Panoramic Highway. Turn right onto Panoramic Highway and go three-quarters of a mile to an intersection where you have three choices. A right turn takes you into Mill Valley. A mild left and up the hill takes you to the summit of Tamalpais. A sharp left turn takes you steeply down to Muir Woods. Take the sharp left. After about a mile you will come to the entrance of Muir Woods. Don't take a right there. Continue another 200 yards and turn right into the overflow parking lot.

August 20, 1993   Serpentine
Sun out now, scattered low clouds. Navy jets going over. Joints okay. Popped a couple of Ibuprofen, just in case. No wind. Quiet except for bugs, moving by at great speed.

The conversation at the Hartford Street Zen Center turned to paraphernalia. There, too, the approach was eclectic. Snyder explained.

It is hard to remember exactly what we had. We had a short *shakujo* without the long staff but with a handle that you could shake. A shakujo has a series of metal rings loosely inserted into openings of a patterned metal piece that is attached to a wooden handle. When one shakes it, the rings vibrate against one another percussion style. I know that we took at least one conch, probably two. We took our *juzu* beads, a Buddhist necklace of 108 beads, and bells, which are called *ghantas.* We also had various magical devices; probably had our pockets full of things like bear claws, beads, very syncretistic.

As Snyder went through this list, Whalen occasionally muttered barely audible noises of protest. Some of the instruments he believed he picked up in Japan in 1966 Snyder seemed to think they had with them in 1965. Snyder considered it possible that they borrowed some of them, or that they belonged to Ginsberg or to himself. We had before us a photograph of Whalen in full regalia on a circumambulation performed on April 8, 1968. He thought Snyder was perhaps reading back from that event to the one in 1965.

STAGE 6

The Route. Begin at the junction of Dipsea Trail and Redwood Creek, in the parking annex of Muir Woods, under a California bay, in the presence of two garbage cans. Chant the Great Wisdom sutra, the dharani for removing disasters, and the Four Vows. Cross Redwood Creek and take Dipsea Trail west. Stop at a coastal live oak growing up through a lone outcrop of rock. There repeat the dharani for removing disasters and sing the Heat mantra. Immediately enter the forest again and contour around several creek beds to an outcropping of almost circular rocks on top of a bare hillside, locally known as Cardiac Hill. Along with the dharani for removing disasters, sing the mantra *Hari om namo Shiva,* an invocation of Shiva. Leave the Dipsea Trail, turn northward along the Old Mine Trail to Pan Toll and continue on the Old Mine Trail to Rock Springs. [Old Mine Trail is no longer in use above Pan Toll.] At the base of this mound of rocks and trees, on the side opposite the gravel parking lot, near a concrete cylinder, sing the *Sarasvati* mantra, an invocation of the goddess Sarasvati, in addition to the usual dharani for warding off disaster. Follow Benstein Trail and the Lagunitas Fire Road to Rifle Camp, where a number of redwood picnic tables are distributed among the live oaks. Eat lunch. Head east along the North Side Trail and stop at an extensive outcropping of serpentine rock. With Sargent's cypress, a tree endemic to serpentine, all around, chant the dharani and *Om Shri Maitreya,* an invocation of the Buddha yet to come. Continue following North Side Trail to Collier Spring, one of the few habitats for redwoods on the northern side of the mountain. In the dark shade of the high canopy, chant two dharanis to the trickle of spring water, adding the dharani of the Great Compassionate One, *Daihi Emmon Bukai Jinshu,* to the dharani for removing disasters. After Collier Spring, the North Side Trail winds in and out of small canyons. Mostly forest turns into mostly chaparral. Not far from Inspiration Point, the summit of Tamalpais comes into view. From this direction it is pyramidal and dark with a scrub covering of manzanita and ceanothus. Inspiration Point is a platform-like knob that provides a clear view to the north and east, over the Marin cities of San Anselmo and San Rafael to Mt. St. Helena at the head of Napa Valley. Sing the dharani for removing disasters along with the mantra to Tara, an invocation of the Bodhisattva Tara, a goddess of compassion. From Inspiration Point to the summit of Tamalpais's East Peak is a short but strenuous climb of about eight hundred feet. On the craggy rocks there, repeat the Great Wisdom sutra, the dharani for removing disasters, the dharani of the Great Compassionate One, Om Shri Maitreya, and Hari om namo Shiva. Add to these the Hari Krishna mantra. Take the very steep Throckmorton Trail [no longer in use] and the gravelly Hogback Trail down to the paved parking lot of Mountain Home. Chant the dharani for removing disasters and the *Gopala* mantra for Krishna as a cowherd. Continue the descent via Panoramic and Ocean View trails back to Muir Woods. Chant the Great Wisdom sutra, the dharani for removing disasters, Hari om namo Shiva, Hari Krishna, and the Four Vows. The circumambulation of Mt. Tamalpais is complete.

May 11, 1991   Collier Spring
Stroked the smooth red bark of the Madrone, maybe the most beautiful tree.

Snyder, in his lecture to my class, referred to the circumambulation as a "walking meditation." In an initial letter to Whalen requesting an interview, dated October 23, 1991, I, too, mentioned this term. Whalen corrected me in his reply, dated October 30, 1991: "The circumambulation of 1965 was not done as 'walking meditation' but as a pilgrimage." I reminded Whalen of what he had written in his letter to me. He replied, "I probably thought of it as some sort of ancient magical tradition that preceded the Buddhist or Tantric traditions that came later. I thought of it as more in the shamanic tradition. I think that Gary is right that the ancient magical tradition became, at least in Buddhism, a walking meditation."

He then referred me, as he had done in his letter, to H. Bryon Earhart's *A Religious Study of the Mount Haguro Sect of Shugendo.* Those who practice *Shugendo* are known as *Yamabushi,* which means, to quote Snyder, "those who sleep or hang out in the mountains." They combine the indigenous Japanese religion of Shinto with Buddhism, introduced from India via China. They believe that mountains are the domain of the *kami* ("spirits" or "gods"), the places where, as Whalen put it, the kami "would quite often land when they came down from heaven, the place where they would hang out." Through their ritual activities, the Yamabushi believe that they can make contact with and avail themselves of the power of the kami. At this point Snyder broke in to emphasize how much his conception and execution of the circumambulation of Tamalpais had been influenced by the Yamabushi. "I got my introduction to these things [that is, to religious practices such as circumambulation] from the Yamabushi. I did some Yamabushi excursions while I was in Japan. I brought some of their practice with me, the way you blow the conch and use the rings [the shakujo]."

STAGE 7

May 11, 1991   Inspiration Point
All I could see from Inspiration Point was condensation of air.

Throughout my conversation with Snyder and Whalen I was struck by their playfulness. They chuckled often as they spoke. They laughed fre-

quently with each other. They fooled around with the Yamabushi paraphernalia. They took themselves very seriously and simultaneously were
bemused by what they had done and by what they were now saying. The
circumambulation had been formal, to be sure, but also play. When I com-
mented upon this attitude, they responded,

SNYDER: See, all of those stops on Tamalpais were like playing with the
        being of the mountain, nothing fancy about it.
WHALEN: Certainly *play* is the operative word here, because that is a great
        deal of the feeling.
SNYDER: You don't have to take superstitions literally. Superstitions are
        metaphors for playful ways of seeing the world.

STAGE 8

August 20, 1993   Summit
The vegetation in the distance is civilization. It is rather late in blooming on the
evolutionary tree, but it has been exceedingly successful and is multiplying rapidly.

I was even more curious about ends. Why did Ginsberg, Snyder, and
Whalen want to go around Mt. Tamalpais in an "intentionally ceremonial"
way? One reason was tribute. As Whalen expressed it, "Recognition of this
mountain as something special, recognizing its identity as a wonderful place,
as a place of some power." For Snyder—whose relationship with Tamalpais,
as of 1965, went back more than a quarter of a century, and whose father
hiked its trails before him—respect and gratitude were particularly important. At the conclusion of an interview in 1989, I asked him what Tamalpais
had meant to him.

What Tamalpais first meant to me was a wild place not too far from
the city. I was struck by the scale of it, the amount of country it covered, how much roadless area there was. Its proximity to the ocean,

its central relationship to the whole Bay Area, its way of relating across to Mt. Diablo and up to Mt. St. Helena and to the northern Bolinas Ridge. It seemed wonderfully located. I was fascinated to explore all the different little subsets of it, the redwood canyons, the live oak canyons, the California nutmeg, the different varieties of chaparral, and the different smells.

It also has a very strong memory for me as the place of my first love. The hike I took with Robin [Collins] was a magical trip. It was the first time the two of us had been out together on our own for a few days.

Then, later, when I was doing graduate study at Berkeley, it was a reachable place to get out to and to go up on. It always had its own climate; you could never tell whether you were going to be in the fog. Its own wind. It was a very powerful presence, presenting alternate realities to what is lower down. That's what mountains seem to do.

It also became a familiar place as I began to lead people on hikes there. I took it as a place to introduce people to the mountains. I did the same thing when I lived in Kyoto. Tamalpais had all those functions. It was also a place I went to be alone a few times, stay out there by myself.

Another reason had to do with the making up of ritual. Ritual allows human beings to negotiate with presences beyond the human. It enables practitioners to make meaningful contact with these presences and to appropriate some of their power for human well-being. The phrase "opening the mountain," used by both Snyder and Whalen in their poems, reveals what they wanted the ritual of circumambulation to accomplish. They wanted to open the eyes of the American people to what Robert Plant Armstrong calls "an affecting presence." They wanted to make an opening for Buddhism in American culture. And they wanted to open a door through which future generations could continually enter the mountain.

Snyder and Whalen are quite explicit on these matters. First, Whalen: "Well, you know, I think that in some respect or other it is about getting Buddhist tradition or feeling established in this country, where it is so foreign, where it is so disconnected from anything real. . . . [Circumambulating a mountain] had this tradition that I was aware of, that I had read about, so we were trying it out. It was entertaining, and people might pick up on the idea." In the interview of 1989, Snyder recalled, "I learned about pradakshina in Japan. Remembering my trails around Tam [that he had hiked in the early to mid 1950s] I thought I would consecrate Tamalpais as a sacred mountain for future generations to do the same kind of pilgrimage on."

A third reason was, as Snyder put it, "devotion." This reason interested me the most, and, yet, through the first hour of the interview in the Hartford Street Zen Center, I had been singularly unsuccessful in getting Snyder and Whalen to talk about it. The changing of the tape gave me the chance to reflect on what I did not have from the interview that I wanted. I decided to ask directly, "I'd like for you to talk more about the religious significance of the initial circumambulation." From Whalen I got what I wanted.

I had a student at Naropa [an institute in Boulder, Colorado] one summer.

She said, "I studied Zen for three years."

And I said, "Oh, is that so. Who with?"

She said, "Professor So and So at Such University."

And I said, "Oh, really. What did you do?"

She said, "Well, we read this sutra and that history of Zen."

And I said, "Oh, that's nice."

Actually Buddhism is very physical. Not only is Zen physical, Chinese Buddhism in general is something people *do*. It's a way of living, it's a way of looking at the world, it's a way of being. To me, anyway, there is a great deal to it of *feeling*. About how you feel about things, how you feel about people, and how you feel toward yourself.

It's very complicated and at the same time very straightforward, very simple. So, here is this mountain, which the Native Americans held in some regard, and then here is this Buddhist tradition of going to the mountains and walking around them, meditating, and reciting sutras.

This was something to *do,* something that you actively, physically—
and mentally, of course—do. It's about living, about walking, eating,
looking at things, handling things. How do we handle the things that
we handle? They are not just things. They have their own being, their
own way. They are also, of course, ourselves, in a funny way. There is-
n't any difference between me and this horn. It's all totally wrapped up
into one bubbling, squeaking, transitory mess. What to say? You take
the horn and blow it. And something happens. Your ears tickle. People
wonder what's happened. They ask, "What's that about?"

Snyder picked up the conch and began to blow it. I felt that I understood.

STAGE 9

August 20, 1993   Mountain Home
Marin County sheriff in his green car. Fully armed. A tourist walks up to him.
"A car is over on its side up Panoramic Highway, at that big curve about a mile
from here. The driver is out. Says he's not injured."

Not surprisingly, given both Snyder's and Whalen's emphasis on "doing,"
their poems on the circumambulation of Mt. Tamalpais are, in the main,
records of the event, rather straightforwardly documented (see appendixes
B and C). The stations of the circumambulation provide structure for both
poems. Snyder lists ten to Whalen's eight because the latter counts neither
the beginning nor the ending at Redwood Creek. Both poets describe the
route and list observations, although Snyder is considerably more detailed.
His attention to things is directly in line with his statement about matter and
spirit to Jack Kerouac nine years before on the steps of the Mountain Theater, and illustrates the continuity of his religious vision and the manner in
which that vision finds expression in his poetry.

   Both poets play in their poems, as they played on the journey itself and in
the interview with me. Wasps were abundant at Rifle Camp, where they

had lunch, and Whalen includes in his poem Ginsberg's query about them—"What do wasps do?"—and Snyder's decidedly unscientific reply: "Mess around." This answer might also be apt were we to ask the question, "What do Buddhist poets do on American mountains?" Characteristically, the most emphatic line in Whalen's poem (signaled by the capital letters) refers not to their mission but to his exasperation at the steepness of the climb from Inspiration Point to the summit: "WHERE IS THE MOUNTAIN?" Snyder's humor is gently audible in his report of the pissing cow, in his description of Ginsberg's reaction to the odor of the California Bay, and in his name for the Marin County country club.

By means of metaphor, both Snyder and Whalen communicate to their readers the essential religious purpose of the circumambulation. Mostly these tropes are subtle, as, for example, the several references to the presence of water in the mountains even in a dry season, and Snyder's note that entering the forest from the grassland is "a new state of being." Sometimes the symbolism is more obvious. Snyder gives the title of the book found in the little hut near Rifle Camp, *Harmony,* and Whalen, at the conclusion of his poem, makes explicit the religious implications of a journey from bottom to top, from the dark shade of redwood groves to the bright light of the summit.

> We marched around the mountain, west to east
> top to bottom—from sea-level (chanting dark stream bed
> Muir Woods) to bright summit sun victory of gods and
> buddhas, conversion of demons, liberation of all sentient
> beings in all worlds past present and future.

STAGE 10

Dinner. After the circumambulation, all who want to will stop at El Rebozo's to eat dinner. It is on your right just before Highway 1 intersects Highway 101. Dinners are about $8.00 not counting drink or tip.

May 11, 1991   Redwood Creek, Muir Woods
Back at the start. Reread "This is the last place."

"Philip," I said, "you mentioned a moment ago that Buddhism has to do with how you feel about yourself. By circumambulating Tam, what did you say about yourself?" He replied, "At that time it stopped me from worrying a lot. I was worrying about a whole lot of things right then. I didn't have to worry as long as I was busy walking around the mountain. So I could feel relatively at ease with myself. I was able just to open up to things and see them and feel comfortable, instead of feeling that I'm no good, or that I'm great. You're just there. A part of the scene."

Coming
Round the
Mountain

AFTER

Included in the liturgy of many ritual celebrations is a retelling of the founding event, the event that gave rise to the ritual. This event may have happened in the period before the present world order, as, for example, at the creation of the world. A part of the ancient Babylonian New Year festival was a narrative rehearsal of the creation of the present world order by Marduk. Or the event may have occurred in history. Readings from the book of Exodus each Passover and a priestly recounting of the Last Supper at every celebration of the Eucharist are well-known examples. Analogously, I believe that the most important function of the poems written by Snyder and Whalen is to provide directions for those who would continue the tradition of ceremonial circumambulation. Considered together, the two poems give precise descriptions of the stations, so that future celebrants can find them, and contain exact lists of the chants. They note features of the terrain, including mention of flora and fauna, implicitly encouraging participants to notice what is around them. And by conveying the attitude of the initial celebrants, they suggest the spirit in which the event should be reenacted.

And reenacted it has been, probably far beyond the wildest expectations of its originators. Snyder and Whalen, either together or separately, have been involved in numerous ceremonies. Neither can remember precisely how many. Snyder estimates that he has done as many as eight. Other people have continued the tradition on their own, most notably Matthew Davis, a Homestead Valley resident and writer, who leads four a year, one at the turn of each season. I have organized a half-dozen or so "circumTams" (Sean O'Grady's phrase) and have participated in others. The first took place on May 19, 1990, when, at my request, Gary Snyder, his wife, Carole Koda, and his son, Kai Snyder, led around the mountain approximately forty-five members of the English department of the University of California, Davis. On several other occasions I have led students in English 184 (Literature of Wilderness) in ceremonial circuits of the mountain.

A major problem in the three pradakshinas I have led has been choice of texts. None of us have been capable of chanting the Hindu and Buddhist sutras and mantras chosen by Snyder, Whalen, and Ginsberg. Only a couple of students out of about two hundred have had any affiliation whatsoever with an Eastern religion. After considerable discussion with the respective classes, and after internal debates with myself about the wisdom of taking the ceremony out of a Hindu/Buddhist context, I have adopted several different ways of dealing with this problem. Sometimes I have chosen a sampling of American poetry to be read at the various stations. Students have been virtually unanimous in their opinion that these texts have not been successful. Sometimes I have used portions of Snyder's poem "The Circumambulation of Mt. Tamalpais" together with materials created by the students themselves. Sometimes there have been no readings. In their place I have encouraged silent meditation and journal writing.

It was not so difficult to find verses that addressed specific powers in the landscape, such as rocks, trees, and flowers. Nor was it all that hard to find spells designed to repel evil and attract good. But finding examples in American English that fit the remaining two of Snyder's categories—a text that "expressed the total truth of the Universe" as all participants understood it, and one that allowed us to "dedicate [our] lives to work for the benefit of every other being on earth"—proved daunting indeed. It may be the case that if you cross democracy with religious freedom you get creatures who simply cannot agree on such matters. The idea of silent meditation and private journal writing was partly a response to this problem.

At the Hartford Street Zen Center I raised with Snyder and Whalen the problem of lifting circumambulations outside of the Eastern tradition of pradakshina. Whalen let out a loud moan when I said that perhaps future circumambulations should be performed only in a Hindu/Buddhist manner.

"That makes it awfully difficult," he said. "How do you feel when you are there?"

I replied, "I feel wonderful."

"Well, then, you say, Here I am at Rock Springs and I feel wonderful. Let's hop up and down and sing 'Happy Days Are Here Again.' You don't have to recite some dharani. Sing something you know."

I turned to Snyder and asked for his opinion. "It is too burdensome to say that it must be a Buddhist ritual," he said. "I would rather think that it is open for anyone to be as creative as they like. They can stop at those points we stopped at, or they can stop at other points. The main thing is to pay your regards, to play, to engage, to stop and pay attention. It's just a way of stopping and looking—at yourself too. In a way, that is what ceremony is for."

When my student had asked me in the coffeehouse, "How do I make nature happen to me?" I was unsure how to respond. I wonder how adequate an answer he would consider this: "Do, when *do* is defined by Philip Whalen, when *do* means 'make a ceremony of.'"

CircumTam, Station I #1. 1994. Polaroid Print.

CircumTam, Station III #1. 1994. Polaroid Print.

CircumTam, Station V #2. 1995. Polaroid Print.

True Communionism #5. 1992. Polaroid Print.

MATTERHORN CLIMB

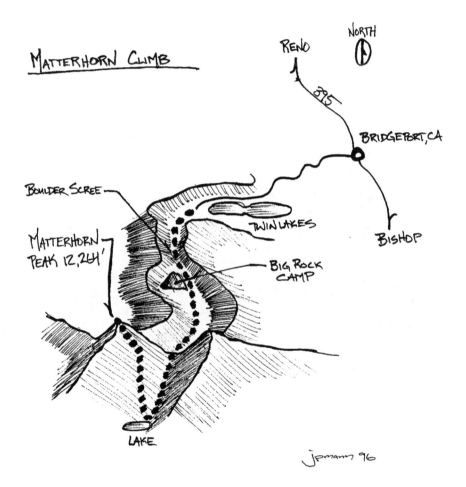

RENO

395

NORTH

BRIDGEPORT, CA

BISHOP

BOULDER SCREE

TWIN LAKES

MATTERHORN PEAK 12,264'

BIG ROCK CAMP

LAKE

jpmann 96

CHAPTER SIX

Real Matter, Real Self

It might very well have been an unsoundness of mind which drove [the Walking Woman] to the open, sobered and healed at last by the large soundness of nature. (Austin 1909, 199)

And beside her go all the Walking People of this book. There is a soundness of nature. Human beings have access to this soundness. One good way to find it is to walk into the wild. Once found, the soundness of nature promotes a soundness of mind. That is, real matter makes for real selves. That these assumptions are true cannot be demonstrated in any conclusive way. As with all creeds that concern the universe and the place of human beings in it, the question is whether they work. That they work can only be discovered by *doing* them.

Human well-being is surely available outside of wild nature. Human history is rich with examples of individuals and communities who find a richness of life without ever venturing into wilderness with body or mind. Human creeds are many, and most of them work satisfactorily for those who practice them consistently. All of the authors in this book are Caucasian Americans with cultural roots in western Europe. This fact is itself sobering and cause for humility. Claims on behalf of Wildness must be grounded in personal histories and proclaimed with appropriate caution.

All creeds can be mispracticed. In particular, what bothers me about "Real Matter, Real Self" is the glee I feel when I leave the trailhead on the way into wilderness. It too much resembles the relief of a man escaping from prison. What if the reverse of conventional wilderness wisdom is actually true? What if the self left behind is the true self and the one "found" in the wild is an inflated self, a bubble floating disembodied in the air somewhere above the mountain tops? From the point of view of this ungrounded self, the structures of the communal, social, economic, and political world might well resemble the walls of a prison. From any other point of view, however, those walls define an arena for responsible action.

Can one get close to real matter with an unreal self? I mean by *real self* our sense of who we really are, deeply and wholly. We have a very difficult time describing this self even to ourselves, but we can usually tell when we have forsaken it. Could it be that the conventional talk about "losing oneself in the wild" is all too accurate? What would happen when unreal self snuggles up to real matter? We who practice the wild tell ourselves that real matter will puncture false feeling and bring unself fizzling to the ground. But I have my doubts.

Ironically, the very movement into the wild, a movement whose intention is to join mind and body in one flesh and fuse matter and spirit into one energy, may end up introducing a new dualism: wilderness out there and home base back here. What is needed is a way to unite there and here, wild and tame, wilderness and city, so that we hikers have our real selves in our packs as we walk on the bedrock of real matter. So that our freedom is grounded in actuality. So that our going out there is coming in here.

The ancient Israelites were among the first in our heritage to discover that escape from bondage did not mean true freedom. Once the Israelites arrived at Sinai, Yahweh announced to Moses that he would descend upon the mountain for all the people to see. It would be on the third day, after the proper ritual preparations had been made. They were to purify themselves by washing their garments and abstaining from sex. Under no conditions were they to touch the mountain (Exodus 19:10–15). Then, "On the morning of day three, thunder came, and lightning. A thick cloud was on the mountain, and a loud trumpet blasted. Yahweh came down upon it in fire. Smoke rose like smoke from the mouth of a furnace, and the whole mountain shook (Exodus 19:16, 18). (All quotations from the Bible in this chapter are my own paraphrases into modern American English. They are not, strictly speaking, accurate translations.) Moses left the people at the base of Sinai and climbed to the top. He came back with the Ten Commandments (Exodus 20:1–17) and several chapters full of social and religious laws (Exodus 21–25), which scholars today call "The Covenant Code."

Yahweh, as Moses and the Israelites first met him at Sinai, was a wild god of arid mountains who revealed himself as thunderstorm and volcano. The laws he dictated to Moses, however, had little to do with the wild. Few, if any, were derived from what we would call desert ecology or from human adaptation to little rain. In context and in content, Yahweh's laws looked forward to the Promised Land. They instructed his people how to behave once they became a nation-state of towns and small cities with an agrarian economy. That is, the Israelites, as described in the book of Exodus, were a people in the wilderness without being of it. Yahweh lived on a mountain but did not inhabit it. His laws were promulgated in arid land but applied, for the most part, to farmland.

While the story of the Israelites at Sinai is troubling to a modern proponent of Wildness like myself, it has some redeeming characteristics. For example, what is, unquestionably, a deficit (separation of land and law) is, at least partly, an asset (connection of wilderness with civilization). Here is the plot, pared down to the weight-bearing bones. A human being goes into the wilderness, climbs a high mountain, and comes down with laws governing, on the one hand, human relations with the cosmos, and, on the other, human relations with each other anywhere and everywhere. Not just on the mountain but on the plain. Not just in the wilderness but in the city. Not just out in the desert but back on the farm. Surely this plot is structurally sound. How sound it is can be tested by contrasting the course of events in Exodus to the plot implicit in the following conversation. The actual scene is Davis, California, where I live, but it could be in Any City, USA:

"Have a good weekend?"

"Great!"

"Where'd you go?"

"Yosemite. Climbed Matterhorn Peak. No one there but me and my friends. Got away from it all. The sky was clear. The air was still. I felt in tune with the universe."

"Wow! I bet you hated to come back to the university."

"Yeah. Same old routine. By this time in the week my neck is stiff, my back hurts, and my sinuses are all clogged. And this weekend it's nothing but work around the house. Oh, to get away again!"

Heroes the world over, fictional and nonfictional, leave home and travel out beyond the known into regions wild and scary. They undergo initiations, experience trials and tribulations, endure ordeals, and return, we hope, with a boon for us. Perhaps Western culture has only two paradigmatic heroes. Jesus returned from the wilderness of the grave with a boon having to do with extraordinary life. He brought back life after death. Moses, on the other hand, came back from the wilderness of Sinai with a boon for ordinary life. He descended from the mountain heights with instructions on how to live life on the plain. The heroes described in *Real Matter* are of Moses' party, with some important differences. Their boons are gifts from the earth itself, not from heaven. Their boons do not come wrapped as commandments, but as suggestions from one human being to another.

Ludlow, Muir, King, Kerouac, Austin, Snyder, and Whalen all believe that soundness resides in this universe, not the one next door. This belief entails an insistence on Wildness, for the universe is, for them, inherently wild. It "elud[es] analysis" and is "beyond categories, self-organizing, self-informing, playful, surprising, impermanent, insubstantial, independent, complete, orderly, unmediated, freely manifesting, self-authenticating, self-willed, complex, quite simple" (Snyder 1990, 10).

This belief also entails an insistence on matter, because the universe is inherently matter/energy. The matter that is most real for them is natural, when natural means not human made. Thus, the importance of heading out on trails. Hiking in wilderness is perhaps a modern, Western, Euro-American label for an age-old practice: the vision quest. Evidently, human beings as a species feel the need to get away from home to accrue certain kinds of power. Being alone is good. Going far is good. The farther the distance travelled, the greater the power accrued. There is, therefore, no substitute for the real physical act of getting oneself into an actual wild place.

A quest for vision, however, is not supposed to be a one-way trip. The power gained is always for use back home—to heal, to inspire, and to guide the questor's own community. So it was with ancient heroes, and so it is with those who are on the trail of new (and renewed) visions for our times and places. Because people like Snyder are so thoroughly "nature mystics," it is easy to conclude that they believe Wildness is available only outside the city limits, even beyond the fences of farm and pasture. But remember the Hershey Bars! Snyder and Kerouac went off on trails through land remarkably wild, given its proximity to urban development. Yet the wildest act of the two-day trip took place after they were back within the limits of Mill Valley.

Kerouac's *Dharma Bums* affirms that the universe will sustain you, not that it will sustain you only if you are hanging on the side of a mountain. When you are in the desert, it is more obvious than anywhere else that the land sets the limits. But the land makes the laws everywhere. You can *do* by making a pradakshina around Mt. Tamalpais. You can also circumambulate the Statue of Liberty or Disneyland. Wildness inhabits every pore of the world, from quarks to galaxies, from stomach pits to cerebral cortexes. The heart of the universe pumps Wildness through all arteries, from backcountry trails to urban avenues. All dualisms, therefore, are inadequate, including the one that places wilderness and home poles apart. The goal of errands into the wilderness is the joining of human communities with all other communities inside the great home that is the universe itself.

In the narratives from the book of Exodus, Yahweh was not really a god of the wilderness, even though his base camp was there. In the final analysis, he required that the prophet and people have faith in him, not in wild nature. Wilderness was sojourn, not journey's ending. His ultimate intention was to move himself and his people north into a beneficent pastoral landscape. The city of Jerusalem eventually supplanted the desert of Sinai as Yahweh's dwelling, and on a hill within its walls Solomon built a temple for him. Even after that, as the story of Elijah in I Kings illustrates, wilderness could still be refuge. If troubles developed in the land of promise, Yahweh was willing for his beleaguered lieutenants to flee there. They must not remain, however. After he clarified their urban mission, he sent them back (I Kings 18–19).

A century or so after Elijah, the prophet Hosea had a radically new vision of wilderness. He flourished during the third quarter of the eighth century B.C.E. A centuries-old war for Israel's allegiance still raged between Yahweh, a god from the desert, and Baal, an agricultural deity. That the Israelites were tempted to worship Baal is easy to understand. During the twelfth century B.C.E. they had entered Palestine primarily as shepherds. They settled originally in the hill country, where they found ample pastures for their sheep. With some exceptions they avoided the cities and the sown land. Gradually, they moved down out of the hills and, as they did so, took up farming. The local farmers had for generations worshipped Baal, whose yearly cycle of life was determined by the seasons. He died every fall for the good of the crops and was resurrected in the spring just in time to deliver the germinating rains. He also knew when and how planting and harvesting should be done. As the Israelites migrated from highland to lowland and traded staff for plow, they turned to Baal, naturally enough, the resident authority on farming and the one who supplied the water.

The conflict between Yahweh and Baal, then, was at base a contest between two economies. Relics of the warfare are scattered throughout the

Bible in the form of stories that express a preference for herding over farming. The best-preserved example is found in Genesis 4, where Cain the farmer unjustly kills the shepherd Abel. The prophet Elijah conducted his campaign against Baal out in the open. Swords in hand, the prophetic warriors of Yahweh sought victory by killing off the prophetic soldiers of Baal. Partly the strategy did not work because the kings of Israel and Judah, though anointed by Yahweh, habitually took their wives from kingdoms loyal to Baal. The practice was good diplomacy, but it infuriated traditional Yahwehists. These foreign wives brought Baal and his attendant priests right into the precincts of Yahweh's palace.

Hosea was a genius of considerable magnitude. As is the case with many superbly creative minds, he reconfigured the war with a few breathtakingly simple moves. Before his time, defenders of Yahweh had kept the functions and the personalities of the two gods distinct. Baal was agricultural, Yahweh pastoral. Yahweh was a somewhat stern though solicitous father; Baal, a handsome lover. It was Baal the paramour, together with the sexual nature of some of the rituals performed in his name, that led Yahweh's faithful to describe Israel's attraction to him as harlotry. Hosea, in a brilliant and daring move, married the two gods. He grafted Baal's function and personality onto the function and personality Yahweh already had. Yahweh became farmer and lover without losing the passion for religious order and social justice evident in the laws he dictated to Moses.

Hosea made out of his own marriage a parable of Yahweh's relation to Israel. Hosea, the husband, stands for Yahweh. He married a prostitute by the name of Gomer, who stands for Israel. Their three children were given names indicative of Yahweh's displeasure with his wife's harlotry. The second child, a daughter, was called "Not pitied," and the third, a son, was named "Not my people." Hosea/Yahweh said to his offspring:

> Beg your mother, beg
>> (for she is not my wife,
>> and I am not her husband)

> that she wipe harlotry from her mouth,
>> and adultery from her breasts.

(Hosea 2:2)

The rationale for Israel's wanton acts is clear. In order to ensure her harvests, she worshipped at the altars of Baal scattered throughout the countryside. Because each region had its own local Baal, one could use the plural (*baalim*) as well as the singular when referring to him. "Lovers" in the following passage refers collectively to the local baals.

> She said, "I will chase after my lovers,
>> who give me my bread and water,
>> my wool and flax, my oil and drink."

(Hosea 2:5)

Israel has blundered here, but not for the old reason. It is not that Baal is agricultural, while Yahweh is pastoral, so that Israel has chosen the wrong god and, implicitly, the wrong profession. According to Hosea, Yahweh is the deity responsible for the crops.

> She did not know
>> I was the one who gave her
>> the grain, the wine, and oil.

(Hosea 2:8)

In the verses that immediately follow, the stern face of Yahweh darkens with vengeance.

> I will ruin the vines and the fig trees
>> she referred to when she said,
> "These are the wages
>> my lovers have paid me."

> I will make them revert to forest,
>> and the wild beasts will eat them.
> I will punish her for celebrating Baal festivals
>> when she burned incense to them
> and decked herself out with ring and jewelry,
>> and pursued her lovers,
>> and forgot me.

(Hosea 2:12–13)

Then, in verse 14, his visage suddenly changes. The personality he has just inherited from Baal, thanks to Hosea, is now evident. It is Yahweh the Lover who speaks:

> Look, I will woo her,
>> and escort her into the wilderness,
>> and speak tenderly to her.
> And there I will give back her vineyards.
> And there she will respond as in her youth,
>> when she came out of the land of Egypt.

(Hosea 2:14–15)

But Hosea had a problem. Fertility rites were an integral part of the Baal liturgy. Surely Yahweh the Father, the Lawgiver, would never permit such ceremonies in his sanctuaries, nor would the more conservative of his followers condone them. If Hosea has let the lover in, can he keep promiscuity out? He needed a way to distinguish between legitimate and illegitimate sex, and he found a pun to do just that. Biblical Hebrew has two words for husband. One is *ish*, which combines the meanings of the word *man* in English and *Mann* in German. The other is *ba'al,* roughly equivalent to the English word *master.* A woman of Hosea's time could designate her husband by saying either *ishi* or *ba'ali.* But, of course, and here is where the pun comes in, *ba'al* is also the word for Yahweh's rival. So, Yahweh says to Israel, once they have returned to the wilderness for a second honeymoon,

> You will call me, "My husband," (*ishi*).
> You will no longer call me, "My husband" (*ba'ali*).
>
> (Hosea 2:16)

Sex with Israel's *ba'al* is wrong. Sex with Israel's *ish* is right. Consummation follows, subtly described by Hosea by means of another pun (the verb "to know" in Hebrew means "to know spiritually" and "to know carnally"):

> On that day I will make a treaty between you and the wild beasts, the air-borne birds, and the animals that creep along the ground. I will break the bow and the sword, and banish war from the land. And I will make you lie down in safety. I promise you a marriage that endures forever. I promise you a marriage full of righteousness and justice, of love and mercy. I promise to be faithful in marriage. And you will know Yahweh. (Hosea 2:18–20)

Return to wilderness in Hosea goes against the grain of travel in the Bible as a whole, where the main direction is toward an urban landscape. The biblical story, after beginning in an earthly garden, and after making a crooked way through many wildernesses, moral as well as natural, ends in a heavenly metropolis, where only those with the mark of the domesticated lamb will be admitted. In Revelation, history ends in eternal city. In Hosea, on the other hand, the story ends with two lovers honeymooning in a real desert. Quite possibly Hosea gives us the earliest recorded vision of wilderness as natural paradise.

I would like to count myself a member of Hosea's party. I, too, have a vision of wilderness as paradise. Our versions are similar. Mine is less optimistic. Nothing will endure forever, except perhaps the universe itself. The universe is good habitat, not a perfect place. Mine is more ecological. For all to lie down in safety would mean somebody goes hungry. So harmony has to go. I would have all of us sign a treaty of relatedness. In it we would declare our faith in an interwoven world. We would vow to do simple acts of kindness and crazy things like walking miles around mountains. We would count on the universe to sustain us. And we would come to know Wildness.

Real Matter,
Real Self

The Heart of the Perfection of the Great Wisdom Sutra
(*Maha Prajna Paramita Hrdaya Sutra*)

The following translation was a joint effort by several people. It is the version used at the Ring of Bone Zendo, San Juan Ridge, Nevada County, California. (Numbers refer to notes at the end of the text.)

Avalokiteshvara Bodhisattva,[1] practicing deep prajna paramita,
clearly saw that all five skandhas[2] are empty, transforming
    all suffering and distress.
Shariputra,[3] form is no other than emptiness, emptiness no
    other than form;
form is exactly emptiness, emptiness exactly form;
sensation, thought, impulse, consciousness are also like this.
Shariputra, all things are marked by emptiness—not born,
    not destroyed;
not stained, not pure; without gain, without loss.
Therefore, in emptiness there is no form, no sensation,
    thought, impulse, consciousness;
no eye, ear, nose, tongue, body, mind;
no color, sound, smell, taste, touch, object of thought;
no realm of sight to no realm of thought;
no ignorance and also no ending of ignorance
to no old age and death and also no ending of old age
    and death;
no suffering, also no source of suffering, no annihilation,
    no path;
no wisdom, also no attainment. Having nothing to attain,
Bodhisattvas live prajna paramita
with no hindrance in the mind. No hindrance, thus no fear.

Far beyond delusive thinking, they attain complete Nirvana.
All Buddhas past, present, and future live prajna paramita
and thus attain anuttara samyak sambodhi.[4]
Therefore, know that prajna paramita is
the great mantra, the wisdom mantra,
the unsurpassed mantra, the supreme mantra,
which completely removes all suffering.
This is truth, not deception.
Therefore, set forth the prajna paramita mantra,
set forth this mantra and say:
"Gate, gate, paragate, parasamgate, bodhi svaha!"[5]

The following notes are from an interview with Gary Snyder, July 22, 1992:

1. "Avalokiteshvara is the Bodhisattva of Compassion. Bodhisattva or Awakening Being is a special term in Mahayana Buddhism for an enlightened being who has dedicated himself to work on behalf of all sentient beings and to live in the world of suffering for however long it takes until all beings have become enlightened together."

2. *Skandhas* are "the five components of an individual organism in Buddhist psychology."

3. *Shariputra* "is the person to whom this sutra is addressed. He was one of the historical disciples of the Buddha."

4. *Anuttara samyak sambodhi* is "highest perfect enlightenment."

5. Snyder's translation of the final line is: "Gone, Gone, Gone Beyond, Gone Beyond Beyond, Awakening, Hail."

"The Circumambulation of Mt. Tamalpais"
by Gary Snyder

Walking up and around the long ridge of Tamalpais, "Bay Mountain" circling and climbing—chanting—to show respect and clarify the mind. Philip Whalen, Allen Ginsberg, and I learned this practice in Asia. So we opened a route around Tam. It takes a day.

STAGE ONE

Muir Woods: the bed of Redwood Creek just where the Dipsea Trail crosses it. Even in the dryest season of this year some running water. Mountains make springs.

> Prajñāpāramitā-hridaya-sūtra
> Dhāranī for Removing Disasters
> Four Vows

Splash across the creek and head up the Dipsea Trail, the steep wooded slope, and into meadows. Gold dry grass. Cows—a huge pissing, her ears out, looking around with large eyes and mottled nose. As we laugh. "—Excuse us for laughing at you." Hazy day, butterflies tan as grass that sit on silver-weathered fenceposts, a gang of crows. "I can smell fried chicken" Allen says—only the simmering California laurel leaves. The trail winds crossed and intertwining with a dirt jeep road.

TWO

A small twisted ancient live oak splitting a rock outcrop an hour up the trail.

Dhāraṇī of Removing Disasters
The Heat Mantra

A tiny chörten before this tree.

Into the woods. Maze fence gate. Young douglas fir, redwood, a new state of being. Sun on madrone: to the bare meadow knoll. (Last spring a bed of wild iris about here and this time too, a lazuli bunting.)

THREE

A ring of outcropped rocks. A natural little dolmen-circle right where the Dipsea crests on the ridge. Looking down a canyon to the ocean—not so far.

Dhāraṇī for Removing Disasters
Hari Om Namo Shiva

And on to Pan Toll, across the road, and up the Old Mine Trail. A doe and a fawn, silvery gray. More crows.

FOUR

Rock Springs. A trickle even now—

The Sarasvatī Mantra
Dhāraṇī for Removing Disasters

—in the shade of a big oak spreading out the map on a picnic table. Then up the Benstein trail to Rifle Camp, old food-cache boxes hanging from wires. A bit north, in the oak woods and rocks, a neat little saddhu hut built of dry natural bits of woods and parts of old crates; roofed with shakes and black plastic. A book called *Harmony* left there. Lunch by the stream, too tiny a trickle, we drink water from our bota. The food offerings are swiss cheese sandwiches, swede bread with liverwurst, salami, jack cheese, olives, gomoku-no-moto from a can, grapes, panettone with apple-currant jelly and sweet butter, oranges, and soujouki—greek walnuts in grape-juice paste. All in the shade, at Rifle Camp.

FIVE

A notable serpentine outcropping, not far after Rifle Camp.

> Om Shri Maitreya
> Dhāranī for Removing Disasters

SIX

Collier spring—in a redwood grove—water trickling out a pipe.

> Dhāranī of the Great Compassionate One

California nutmeg, golden chinquapin the fruit with burrs, the chaparral. Following the North Side Trail.

SEVEN

Inspiration point.

> Dhāranī for Removing Disasters
> Mantra for Tārā

Looking down on Lagunitas. The gleam of water storage in the brushy hills. All that smog—and Mt. St. Helena faintly in the north. The houses of San Anselmo and San Rafael, once large estates . . . "Peacock Gap Country Club"—Rocky brush climb up the North Ridge trail.

EIGHT

Summit of Mt. Tamalpais. A ring of rock pinnacles around the lookout.

Prajñāpāramitā–hridaya–sūtra
Dhāranī for Removing Disasters
Dhāranī of the Great Compassionate One

Hari Krishna Mantra
Om Shri Maitreya
Hari Om Namo Shiva

All around the bay, such smog and sense of heat. May the whole planet not get like this.
Start the descent down the Throckmorton Hogback trail. (Fern Canyon an alternative.)

NINE

Parking lot of Mountain Home. Cars whiz by, sun glare from the west.

Dhāranī for Removing Disasters
Gopala mantra.

Then, across from the California Alpine Club, the Ocean View Trail goes down. Some yellow broom flowers still out. The long descending trail into shadowy giant redwood trees.

TEN

The bed of Redwood creek again.

Prajñāpāramitā-hridaya-sūtra
Dhāranī for Removing Disasters
Hari Om Namo Shiva
Hari Krishna Mantra
Four Vows

—standing in our little circle, blowing the conch, shaking the staff rings, right in the parking lot.

ॐ

APPENDIX C

Opening the Mountain, Tamalpais:22:x:65
by Philip Whalen

Hot sunny morning, Allen and Gary, here they come, we are
ready.
Sutras in creek-bed, chants and lustrations, bed of Redwood
Creek
John Muir's Woods.

First Shrine: Oak tree grows out of rock
                  Field of Lazuli Buntings, crow song

Second Shrine: Trail crosses fire road at hilltop
                  Address to the Ocean
                  Siva music addressed to the peaks

Third Shrine: Rock Springs music for Sarasvati
                  Remember tea with Mike and JoAnn years ago
                  Fresh water in late dry season

Fourth Shrine: Rifle Camp lunch, natural history:
                  Allen: "What do wasps do?"
                  Gary: "Mess around."

Fifth Shrine: Collier Spring, Great Sharani & Tara music

Sixth Shrine: Inspiration Point, Gatha of Vajra
                  Intellectual
                  Heat lightning

To the Summit: North Side Trail, scramble up verticl

North

Knee WHERE IS THE MOUNTAIN?

Seventh Shrine: the Mountain top: Prajnaparamita Sutra, as

many

others as could be remembered in music &

song

Eighth Shrine: The parking lot, Mountain Home

Sunset Amida going West

O Gopala, &c Devaki Nandi na Gopala

with a Tibetan encore for Tara,

Song against disaster.

Return to Creekbed, Muir Woods: Final Pronouncement of the
Sutras

We marched around the mountain, west to east
top to bottom—from sea-level (chanting dark stream
bed
Muir Woods) to bright summit sun victory of gods and
buddhas, conversion of demons, liberation of all sentient
beings in all worlds past present and future.

LITERATURE CITED

Adams, Ansel

1949   *My Camera in Yosemite.* Yosemite: Virginia Adams and Boston: Houghton Mifflin.

Armstrong, Robert Plant

1971   *The Affecting Presence.* Urbana: University of Illinois Press.

Austin, Mary

1903   *The Land of Little Rain.* Boston and New York: Houghton Mifflin.

1909   *Lost Borders.* New York and London: Harper and Brothers.

Baer, William

1856   "A Trip to the Yosemite Falls." *Mariposa Democrat,* Aug. 5, 1856. Reprinted in *California Historical Society Quarterly* 1 (1922–23): 271–85.

Cohen, Michael P.

1984   *The Pathless Way: John Muir and American Wilderness.* Madison: University of Wisconsin Press.

Danley, L. E.

1908   "To Yosemite in a Modern Observation Passenger Car." *The Grizzly Bear* 3.

Earhart, H. Bryon

1970   *A Religious Study of the Mount Haguro Sect of Shugendo.* Tokyo: Sophia University.

Kerouac, Jack

1957   *On the Road.* New York: Viking Press.

1958   *Dharma Bums.* New York: Viking Press.

King, Clarence
1864   "California Geological Survey." In Clarence King papers, Henry E. Huntington Library, San Marino, Calif.
1872   *Mountaineering in the Sierra Nevada.* Boston: James R. Osgood & Co.

172

Lehmer, O. W.
n.d.   *Yosemite National Park.* Chicago: Poole Brothers, Printers.

Ludlow, Fitz Hugh
1857   *The Hasheesh Eater.* New York: Harper and Brothers.
1864   "Seven Weeks in the Great Yo-Semite." *Atlantic Monthly* 13:739–54. Reprinted in *The Heart of the Continent* (New York: Hurd & Houghton, 1870).

Muir, John
1911a   *Mountains of California.* New and enlarged edition. New York: The Century Co.
1911b   *My First Summer in the Sierra.* Boston: Houghton Mifflin.

Nicosia, Gerald
1983   *Memory Babe.* New York: Grove Press.

Morse, Cora
1896   *Yosemite As I Saw It.* San Francisco: San Francisco News Co.

O'Grady, John P.
1993   *Pilgrims to the Wild.* Salt Lake City: University of Utah Press.

Richardson, Albert

1867   *Beyond the Mississippi.* Hartford: American Publishing Co.

Russell, William H.

1902   *Herperothen: Notes from the West: A Record of a Ramble in the United States and Canada in the Spring and Summer of 1901.* London: Sampson, Low, Marston, Seurles, & Rivington.

Snyder, Gary

1954–56 Journals. Unpublished.

1983   Personal interview, Oct. 6.

1989   Personal interview, Apr. 26.

1990   *The Practice of the Wild.* San Francisco: North Point Press.

1991   Lecture to English 184, Apr. 23, 1991. Notes taken by Roswitha Muller and Mark Wheelis.

1992a   "On Climbing the Sierra Matterhorn Again After Thirty-one Years." In *No Nature,* p. 362. New York: Pantheon Press.

1992b   Personal interview, July 22.

1996   "Circumambulation of Mt. Tamalpais." In *Mountains and Rivers Without End.* Washington, D.C.: Counterpoint Press.

Snyder, Gary, and Philip Whalen

1992   Personal interview, Mar. 12.

Sussman, Emilie

1872   *My Trip to Yosemite.* San Francisco: n.p.

Whalen, Philip

1969   "Opening the Mountain, Tamalpais: 22:X:65." In *On Bear's Head,* pp. 307–8. New York: Harcourt, Brace & World.

1991   Letter to David Robertson, Oct. 30.

Adams, Ansel, 6
Armstrong, Robert Plant, 133
Austin, Mary: *Land of Little Rain,* ix, x,
    55, 56, 57–58, 59–61, 62–64, 65–68,
    69; *Lost Borders,* ix, 55; retracing the
    trail of, 55, 61, 71–75; on the
    soundness of nature, 68–69;
    sympathies of, 70. *See also* Mesa
    Trail; Walker, Mrs.

Baal, 154–55, 156, 157
Baer, William, 5–6
Bible, 42–43, 44, 138, 150, 154–58
Bierstadt, Albert, 2
Border Inn Motel and Cafe, 92, 94
Brewer, William, 26
Buddhism, 102–3, 111, 133–35. *See also*
    Heart of the Perfection of the Great
    Wisdom Sutra; *Pradakshina*

Carson City, 79–80
Carson Plains, 81–82
Christianity, 44, 111–12. *See also*
    Bible
Church, Frederick, 31
Cohen, Valerie and Michael, 90, 92
Collins, Robin, 101, 133
Cotter, Dick, 27–28
Creeley, Robert, 103
Crockenberg, Vince, 35, 37, 38

Dalenburg, Claude, 103
Danley, L. E., 6
Davis, Matthew, 138

deBit, Ralph Moriarty, 87–88
Dharma, 108

Earhart, H. Bryon, 131
Elijah, 154, 155
El Pueblo de Las Uvas, 63–64

Faith, 44–45
Faulkner, Hal, 35, 37, 38
Fences, 61, 81–82
Forgang, David, 17
Four Vows, 123, 127, 129, 130
Free, John B., 88
Freedom, 69, 150

Ginsberg, Allen, 103, 107, 123, 127, 136
Glasser, Harold, 90, 92
God, 14, 16. *See also* Yahweh

Hammond, Bruce, 35, 36, 37, 38
Heart of the Perfection of the Great
    Wisdom Sutra, 123, 127, 129, 130,
    161–62
Hershey Bars, 105, 113
Highway 50, 76, 78–97
Home Farm, 87–89
Hosea, 154, 155–58
Hoyer, Mark, 90, 92
Hyde, Ellen and Kenneth, 85–86

Jesus, 152
Jimville, 62–63
John Muir Trail, 8–9, 10–14, 16
Jones, D, 90, 92

Kerouac, Jack: Christian perspective of, 111–12; climbs Matterhorn Peak, 35, 36, 38–39, 40; *Dharma Bums,* 36, 38–39, 40, 107–9, 111–12, 153; faith of, 45; hikes around Mt. Tamalpais, 100, 104–5, 108–9, 111–12; *On the Road,* 111

King, Clarence, 43; climb of Mt. Tyndall, 24, 26–28; faith of, 44–45; *Mountaineering in the Sierra Nevada,* 32–33; retracing route of, 29–32; on space, 32–33, 34

King, Roger, 80

Kirk, Andrew, 29, 90, 92

Koda, Carole, 70, 138

Lamantia, Philip, 103

Lehmer, O. W., 5

Ludlow, Fitz Hugh: *The Hasheesh Eater,* 2; *The Heart of the Continent,* 2–4; retracing the route of, 8, 9–23; in Yosemite, 2–5, 6

Lyon, Tom, 35, 36, 37, 38

McClure, Michael, 103

McCorkle, Locke, 101, 102, 103, 125

McKenzie, Leonard, 13

Matter, real, 115, 149, 152; Snyder on, 100, 109, 113, 114

Matterhorn Peak; map, 146; retracing the route of Snyder et al. up, 35–41, 46–51

Mesa Trail: Austin on, 54, 55, 56–58, 62–63; map. 52; retracing Austin on, 55, 61, 71–75

Montgomery, John, 35, 36

Moreno, Rich, 80

Morse, Cora, 6–7

Moses, 42–43, 44, 150, 152

Mountains: faith in, 28–29, 45; value of, 34; walking in, 114. *See also under specific mountain name*

Mt. Hiei, 125, 126

Mt. Moriah, 90, 91–92

Mt. Ritter, 33–34, 41

Mt. Tamalpais: circumambulated by Snyder et al., 123, 124–25, 127–29, 130–36; circumambulation of as ceremonial event, 138–40; Kerouac and Snyder hike around, 100, 104–5, 108–9, 111–12; map, 98; retracing circumambulation of Snyder et al., 120, 123–25, 126–28, 129–30, 138–40, 142–45; retracing Kerouac and Snyder around, 106, 113, 115–19; significance of to Snyder, 100–102, 132–33

Mt. Tyndall, 24, 26, 28, 32–33, 34

Mt. Whitney, 26

Muir, John: climbs Mt. Ritter, 41; faith of, 45; *My First Summer in the Sierra,* 33; quotes of on John Muir Trail, 10, 11; on Sierra Nevada landscape, 33–34

Nature: "secrets" of, in Yosemite, 4–6, 7, 8, 16; soundness of, 68–69, 148

Noel, Paul, 35, 37

Nowhere Cafe, 85–86, 95

Nowick, Walter, 125

O'Grady, Sean, 29, 31–32, 46, 90, 92, 113, 138

Orlovsky, Peter, 103
Owens, Maryann, 90, 92

Past, the, 115
Play, 131–32
Pocket Hunter, 59, 60–61, 62
Pradakshina, 125–26, 131, 134–35

Ransick, Chris, 29
Rexroth, Kenneth, 103
Richardson, Albert, 6, 8
Ritual, 133
Robertson, Jeannette, 78, 90, 92, 93
Rothenberg, David, 90, 92
Russell, W. H., 5

Sarver, Stephanie, 90, 92
Schimmoeller, Katrina, 46
Self, real, 149
Seyavi, 59–60, 62
Shaffer, Eric Paul, 29
Sindt, Chris, 46
Snyder, Gary, 70; association with Mt.
    Tamalpais, 100–102, 107, 132–33;
    circumambulates Mt. Tamalpais,
    123, 124–25, 127–29, 130–34, 138;
    "The Circumambulation of Mt.
    Tamalpais," 135–36, 139, 163–67;
    hikes with Kerouac around Mt.
    Tamalpais, 100, 104–5, 108–9, 111;
    on hiking, 107–10, 114; on *pradak-
    shina,* 125–26, 134, 140; on real
    matter, 100, 109, 113, 114; reclimbs
    Matterhorn Peak, 35, 36, 37, 38, 39,
    40–41; on the universe, 152

Snyder, Kai, 138
Space, 32–33, 34
Sussman, Emilie, 5

Taylor, Val, 87–89
Time, 34

Walker, Mrs. (Walking Woman), 65–68,
    69, 148
Watts, Alan, 103
Welch, Lew, 29
Whalen, Philip, 103, 107; on Bud-
    dhism, 133–35; circumambulates
    Mt. Tamalpais, 123, 124, 125, 127,
    129, 130–32, 137, 139–40; "Open-
    ing the Mountain, Tamalpais:
    22:x:65," 135–36, 168–69
Wheelis, Mark, 35, 36, 37, 38
Wilderness: in the Bible, 112, 158;
    hiking as vision quest, 152–53; as a
    place for testing, 43; united with
    city, 149, 151
Wildness, 14–16, 148, 152, 153
Williams, William Carlos, 100, 103
Winnenap, 59, 60, 62

Yahweh, 42, 43, 150, 154–58
Yamabushi, 131
Yosemite Valley: "closet" metaphor for,
    3, 4; "heart" metaphor for, 6–7; "in-
    accessible" view of, 4–5, 6; Ludlow
    in, 2–5, 6; map, xii; retracing Lud-
    low in, 8–23; "secrets" in, 5–6, 7, 8,
    16. *See also* John Muir Trail; Muir,
    John

ABOUT THE AUTHOR

David Robertson teaches in the English Department, the Program in Nature and Culture, and the Graduate Ecology Group at the University of California, Davis. He is the author of *West of Eden: A History of the Art and Literature of Yosemite* and *Yosemite As We Saw It: A Collection of Early Writings and Art.* He is currently working on bioregional studies of the Yuba River watershed in the Sierra Nevada and the watersheds of Putah and Cache creeks in California's coastal mountains.